CASTLES OF SCOTLAND

IAN GRIMBLE

CASTLES OF SCOTLAND

BBC BOOKS

Published by BBC Books
a division of BBC Enterprises Ltd
Woodlands, 80 Wood Lane, London W12 0TT

ISBN 0 563 20518 0

First published 1987
© Ian Grimble 1987

Set in 11/13 Times by Ace Filmsetting Ltd, Frome, Somerset
and printed in Great Bratain by
St Edmundsbury Press, Bury St Edmunds, Suffolk

CONTENTS

PREFACE

Good companions of former ploys have shared in this one, as well as others with whom 1 have had the pleasure of working for the first time. Barry Toovey, who directed my earlier television series, *Grimble on Islands* and *Houses of Fortune*, was the producer of this one. Linda Woodward, his production assistant, has kept us all in order. Ken Gow, Douglas Campbell and Alastair Black had all seen me ageing in front of their cameras long before we met at these castles. The sound recordists were Stephen Bulfield, Colin Maclure and Alan Cooper. The editors, using a new system that I had not seen before, were Rhona Mitchell and Rob Shortland. Sandy Fraser and Kenny Laird were the lighting electricians: when filming on location, the narrator and electrician are generally well placed to observe that work is the downfall of the drinking classes.

The editor of *Scottish Islands*, Hilary Duguid, has once again remedied many of the faults in the text of this one. I am deeply grateful, though not even she can place what I write beyond the reach of censure.

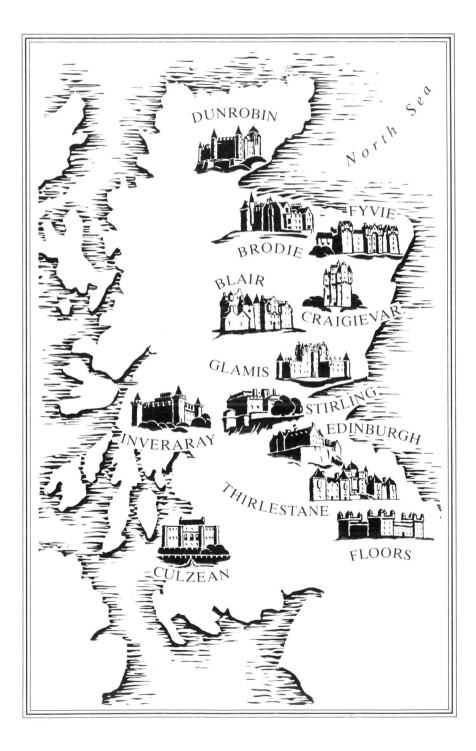

INTRODUCTION

Why these particular twelve castles, anyone might ask? As in the case of islands, the task of making a representative selection for a television series was not an easy one. The first criterion was that they should all be open to the public, but the choice has been limited in other ways. The BBC Scotland television series on islands included Arran, which removed Brodick from the list of eligible subjects. The island documentaries in their turn lost Skye, because Dunvegan had been included in the television series *Houses of Fortune*. To have presented Skye without Dunvegan would have been to enact Hamlet without the Prince. The present series has lost Cawdor and Drumlanrig, in addition to Dunvegan, because all of them were explored in *Houses of Fortune*.

There are castles that enjoy great celebrity on calendars and in tourist brochures, notably Duart on Mull, Eilean Donan in Loch Alsh and Castle Stalker in Loch Linnhe. But these were abandoned ruins until they were restored, and lack the contents necessary to illustrate the details of their history. Others, such as Balnagown in Ross shire, have changed their contents with their ownership, although they were never left derelict. The accident of nomenclature has also exercised its capricious influence on choice. When is a castle not a castle? When it is not called one. Scone Palace is neither more nor less a castle than Floors, and Innes House in Moray might be thought as well entitled to be called a castle as Brodie.

Within the limits imposed by such considerations, we have done our best to present a representative selection. *Houses of Fortune* ran to seven programmes, *Grimble on Islands* to six. Now there are twelve features on castles, which is the final governing factor. The object has been to include castles from every region of Scotland, though this has been frustrated in the last resort by the fact that so many of them, from Muness in Unst to Dunyveg in Islay, are ruins today. From those that remain intact, a choice has been made which attempts to reflect the range of architectural styles that evolved in Scotland. We have tried also to represent the diverse ethnic origins of the folk who settled in this country and achieved the power to build themselves castles as a means of preserving what they had won.

EDINBURGH

Few nations possess a fortress so closely wedded to their country's history or more dramatically situated in the heart of their capital. The outlines of Edinburgh Castle have changed, like its functions, over the centuries, but its magnetism remains undiminished. The hosts of strangers who come to discover Scotland's past find the object of their search in this monument.

It occupies a rock consisting of the core of an extinct volcano, precipitous except on the east side, where a glacier during the Ice Age left its sediment as it eddied round the obstruction. The waters of the Firth of Forth lie to the north, while the Pentland Hills break the horizon to the south. It stands sentinel on the coastal route to the west, where the narrow waist of Scotland was fenced by the Antonine Wall in Roman times. Whatever part it had played before or since then, no evidence remains in the buildings on the rock until the dynasty of Malcolm III and his Queen (canonised in 1251 as Saint Margaret) occupied the throne.

There is no trace of the castle in which Queen Margaret died in 1093, after hearing of the death of her husband and eldest son. But the chapel dedicated to her still stands, though much restored – the earliest surviving structure on the rock. Probably it was established in her memory by her youngest son King David I, after he had succeeded to the throne in 1124. He also may have refounded the church on the summit of the rock, and dedicated it to St Mary. In 1128 he erected the Augustinian abbey of the Holy Rood a mile away to the east.

At the end of the following century the castle became one of the storm centres of the Scottish war of independence. In 1296 Edward I of England began his attempt to conquer Scotland by attacking the frontier town of Berwick, the country's principal port, massacring its inhabitants including the women and children. He then captured and garrisoned Edinburgh Castle, which became henceforth one of the most frequently besieged strongholds in Europe. Again and again it changed hands during the years of struggle against the English, until Sir Thomas Randolph recovered it in 1313, shortly before the Battle of Bannockburn. A plaque on the castle walls commemorates his feat, though these are not the walls he saw. King Robert the Bruce demolished those entirely, lest the castle should ever again become the headquarters for an English occupation.

It was the Bruce's son David II who substantially refortified the castle after his succession in 1329, with defensive walls covering the approach on the most vulnerable side of the rock. At intervals his Stewart successors added more commodious living quarters behind King David's protective tower. James I, the poet-king, returned in 1424 from his long captivity in England and built himself a hall of which no trace remains today.

A few decades later the castle was the scene of a grizzly episode during the minority of his son James II, when his guardians decided to take drastic measures against the over-mighty house of Douglas. The earldom of Douglas had been inherited by a sixteen-year-old youth, whom they invited with his younger brother to dine with the ten-year-old King in the hall his father had erected. According to tradition, a black boar's head was served, the symbol of a death sentence. The young Douglases were then dragged from their seats, and executed without further formality in the courtyard. Before the age of the popular press, there were other means of publishing such scandals:

> *Edinburgh Castle, Town and Tower,*
> *God grant thou sink for sin,*
> *And that even for the black dinner*
> *Earl Douglas gat therein.*

James II married Mary of Gueldres, whose uncle the Duke of Burgundy ruled over one of the most prosperous and civilised provinces of Europe. It was this alliance that endowed Scotland with the castle's most celebrated piece of ordnance, a bombard manufactured in the 1440s, probably at Mons in what is now Belgium, and known as Mons Meg. It was to prove an effective means of establishing the royal authority, since it could batter down the stoutest walls of obstreperous subjects. Weighing six and a half tons, it required 100 horses and men to move it an average of less than four miles a day.

By the end of the Middle Ages the function of the royal hall was changing. More private apartments were being built around it, so that it was not required for the communal life-style of a less sophisticated era. It came to be reserved increasingly for ceremonial purposes. In these circumstances, James IV, after he became king in 1488, commissioned the building of a more splendid hall in the castle. It is a fitting memento of this forward-looking king, the founder of the first faculty of medicine at any university in Britain in his new college at Aberdeen, and of the Royal College of Surgeons in Edinburgh.

James IV's passion for building was cut short by his death on the field of Flodden in 1513, but his fine hall had been completed. Perched above its precipice, it looks sufficiently remarkable today, seen from below. Those who witnessed its construction from their mean dwellings at the foot of the rock in about 1500 must have been filled with wonder.

Massive vaults had first to be built down the craggy slope of the volcanic cone, to provide a flat platform for the great hall. It was lit by four large windows facing south, its roof supported by a hammer-beam timber framework of superb design. To the east of the hall other palace buildings rose above similar vaults clinging to the steep rock.* The palace buildings surround what became known as Crown Square, whose fourth side, opposite the new hall, was occupied by the mediaeval church of St Mary.

From 1529 James V also began building a palace (known as Holyroodhouse) beside the abbey of the Holy Rood. The earliest part of it is the north-west tower, rectangular with round corner towers, four storeys crowned by a crenellated parapet and a gabled roof within it. A wing extended from the tower, but without a matching tower beyond it. Like everything else in Edinburgh, it was exposed to the fury of Henry VIII of England when James V died in 1542, leaving a week-old baby as the Queen of Scots.

Henry, her nearest male relative, demanded that the baby Queen Mary should be sent to England and betrothed to his son Edward. When he was thwarted, the Rough Wooing commenced, according to the following instructions: 'Put all to fire and sword. Burn Edinburgh town, so razed and defaced when you have sacked and gotten what you can of it as there may remain for ever a perpetual memory of the vengeance of God. Beat down and overthrow the castle, sack Holyroodhouse.'

The new palace was damaged in the invasion of 1544 but not destroyed. Happily, while the English failed to capture the castle, they made a most valuable sketch of it, the only record of its appearance before King David II's tower was demolished. In the aftermath

---

* To the west of the hall an Artillery House is recorded in 1498.

of the terror and destruction, the widowed Queen Mary of Lorraine built a palace for herself on the side of the castle hill. This fine Renaissance building was demolished in 1846 to make room for the premises of the Free Church of Scotland in which the General Assembly meets today.

One of the most interesting souvenirs of the reign of James V and his Queen to have escaped English malice and religious zeal is a pair of royal coats-of-arms in stained glass in a window of the Magdalen chapel in the Cowgate, now the university's Chaplaincy Centre. The chapel was founded in 1541 by the burgess Michael Maquhen and his wife Janet, with an endowment to relieve destitution and illness. Their armorials are preserved in the same window. These are the only specimens of pre-Reformation stained glass of any importance to have survived in Scotland.

Janet was widowed at about the same time as Mary of Lorraine, and it appears likely that the armorials were a gift from the Queen, a gesture of respect and sympathy from one devout woman to another. In the castle, a wall of the palace building displays a modern plaque containing the Queen Regent's family device on a lozenge, and commemorates her death here in 1560. In the following year her daughter Mary Queen of Scots arrived from France to embark on her personal reign.

Queen Mary showed a preference for the palace of Holyroodhouse when she resided in Edinburgh, though she did choose the castle when she gave birth to her son. Here, the date of the event is marked by an inscription above one of the entrances, where the cipher MAH, Mary and Henry, formerly Lord Darnley, appears with the numerals 1566. Within, the little room in which James VI first saw the light is still to be seen, the same date among its painted decorations. In the following year his mother was deposed.

After her flight into England, the gallant Sir William Kirkcaldy of Grange held the castle in her name against those who ruled on behalf of her infant son. From May 1568 until the spring of 1573 the fortress proved unassailable. Then Queen Elizabeth of England, who had made a captive of her cousin and heir, and promoted the dissemination of outrageous libels against her character throughout Europe, once again sent an invading force to Scotland in support of her enemies.

Elizabeth despatched an army conducting twenty great guns with expert marksmen, who battered down the castle's defences, including

King David's tower. Kirkcaldy of Grange surrendered on honourable terms, only to be hanged ignominiously in public. 'Unless he forsake that wicked course wherein he is entered,' John Knox had predicted, 'he shall be pulled out of that nest, and his carcase hang before the sun.' This was not the first time one of his prophecies received a gruesome fulfilment through the agency of the Queen of England.

The castle had sustained comparatively little damage during the Rough Wooing. It was the monasteries and private dwellings that had borne the brunt of Henry VIII's anger and frustration. Now David II's tower was in ruins, and its stones were used in the construction of a great semi-circular battery, protecting the palace behind it. From the half-moon battery a defensive wall, incorporating what remained of the older fortifications, was built to the entrance gate, likewise repaired. On this a memorial plaque has been placed in honour of Sir William Kirkcaldy of Grange. So the castle began to assume the appearance it presents to those who visit it today.

But henceforth its functions changed, as it ceased to be used as a royal residence and was adapted gradually to serve the purposes of a military garrison. James VI spent much of his youth in Stirling Castle, and in Edinburgh he preferred the amenities of Holyroodhouse. It was from here that he rode south in 1603 to occupy the throne of England, after the death of Elizabeth. He paid only one visit to his Scottish kingdom during the remainder of his life, in 1616, when part of the palace range in the castle was enlarged before his arrival. No monarch entered it again until Charles I came in 1633 to be crowned King of Scots.

It was Charles who ordered the building of the Parliament House, designed as the seat of the College of Justice. This new hall was to be even more magnificent than that built by James IV in the castle. Work began on its construction in 1632, on a site close to the church of St Giles, and it took over seven years to complete. By then King Charles was faced by open rebellion and could afford no contribution to its cost, so that it was borne entirely by the Town Council and citizens of Edinburgh. The College of Justice assembled in it for the first time in 1642, the year in which Charles first raised his standard at Nottingham to fight the English Parliamentarians.

Oliver Cromwell established a military dictatorship in Scotland in 1651, after Charles II's attempt to recover his father's crown had been defeated at the Battle of Worcester. The castle was now adapted to serve the needs of a Commonwealth garrison. The mediaeval church of St Mary, which James IV had converted into a Munition House, was enlarged to serve as a powder magazine, while the chapel of St Margaret became the munitions store. The great hall of James IV was partitioned to accommodate the troops. These same soldiers were set to work, digging a deep ditch as additional protection for the castle entrance on the gentle slope below which the esplanade lies today.

Cromwell's Council for Scotland met in the palace of Holyroodhouse in 1658, and after the restoration of Charles II in 1660, the king commissioned Sir William Bruce to rebuild the palace on a far grander scale. The old tower was retained, and a second one resembling it was built at the other end of the façade, thus fulfilling the original intention of the previous century.

The façade itself was built anew, in the same classical Renaissance style as the courtyard behind, with its three architectural orders. King Charles laid down his requirements with precision: 'He will only have his own great apartments to the east upon the new privy garden, and the old royal apartment where it now is, the privy chamber of it being enlarged as is proposed, and the drawing room and bed chamber to be as it now is in the north tower.' Thus he preserved the rooms which had witnessed the murder of Rizzio, Queen Mary's secretary and, her enemies asserted, her lover.

Charles II never visited the palace himself, but sent his brother the Duke of York to Scotland as his Lord High Commissioner in 1680. James settled into Holyroodhouse, installed a Catholic chapel in the picture gallery, and embarked on the restoration of the abbey church.

In November 1681 the Duke, who was a professed Catholic, was compromised by the Scottish Privy Council when it moved against that staunch opponent of Catholicism, the ninth Earl of Argyll, charging him with treason on evidence which, as an Englishman declared openly, 'they would not hang a dog upon'. After his conviction he was lodged in Edinburgh Castle, while the verdict was sent to the King in London. Expecting a death sentence, the Earl's step-daughter Lady Sophia Lindsay obtained permission to pay him a farewell visit. She arrived at about seven in the evening, attended by a servant carrying a large lantern. The page who bore her train, to protect it from the muddy streets, wore a fair wig and had his head bandaged as if he had been injured in a brawl. The guards heard Lady Sophia taking a tearful farewell, then the party walked out again into the night.

6

The great gate was opened, and here one of the guards took the page by the arm and scrutinized him. The lantern carrier expostulated over the delay while Lady Sophia twitched her train so that it fell out of the page's hands into the mire. She rounded on him angrily and the guard, vexed by all this fuss, allowed them to proceed. At the foot of the castle hill Lady Sophia's servants abandoned her, running down to the Grassmarket where horses were waiting. Only when they reached Craigmillar Castle did the Earl pause to exchange his page's costume for more appropriate riding clothes.

He took refuge in Holland, but returned on James VII's accession in 1685, to take part in the attempt to make the Duke of Monmouth, Charles II's bastard son, king in James's place. Argyll was captured in Scotland, and this time he was placed in irons in the castle before his execution. He is commemorated by the name of the Argyle tower that surmounts the old portcullis entrance, though this was built centuries after his death.

During his brief reign, James VII revived the Most Noble Order of the Thistle, intending that the restored abbey church should serve as the chapel of the Order. By 1688 altars had been erected in the old nave, and stalls for the Knights of the Thistle. Since this church had formerly served the parishioners of the Canongate, he built them another parish church, whose attractive Dutch exterior still faces the Royal Mile.

The abbey church was less fortunate. As soon as Dutch William was known to have landed in England, a Protestant mob broke into Holyroodhouse to vandalize the royal chapel in the picture gallery. They then entered the ancient edifice which housed the chapel of the Thistle, where they even broke into the royal burial vault and cast out the bones of dead kings. A bonfire in the outer court was heaped with service books, vestments and effigies. The roof of the desecrated church collapsed in 1758.

In the castle, the Duke of Gordon held out on behalf of James VII until 13 June 1690, when his garrison consisted of only eighty-six men, their fire power thirty barrels of powder to feed twenty-two pieces of artillery. The men suffered from scurvy and ill-dressed wounds while their supply of food and water dwindled. Finally the Jacobite Duke raised the white flag of surrender. He took leave of his men on the parade ground, thanking them for their courage and loyalty, and distributing money to them to pay the expenses of their journey home. The surrender terms guaranteed full liberty to each of them, but as soon as they had marched out of the castle, the Duke was hustled away under guard while he could see his men being lynched by the mob.

The continuing Jacobite threat moved the government to strengthen the castle's defences during the reign of Queen Anne, so the military engineer Theodore Dury was sent to Edinburgh in 1708. He improved the southern walls and constructed new batteries at either end of them. One is known as the Butts Battery because it was placed on the site of the old archery butts; while the other, at a higher level, is called Dury's Battery. A long flight of steps connects the two levels.

Hardly were these works completed when Queen Anne died in 1714, to be succeeded by her cousin George of Hanover. There followed the uprising in the name of the Old Pretender, Queen Anne's half-brother, *de jure* King James VIII. A party of young men planned to capture the castle in his name, aided by a sentry on duty where the walls of the western defences overlook crags and steeply sloping ground.

When the man who was to have brought rope ladders failed to appear, the rest of the group climbed the rock without him, in order not to be late for their assignation. They threw up a rope that they carried with them, but it proved to be too short. Then the watch appeared on the parapet above, making its rounds before the appointed time. The sentry sounded the alarm, both to warn the conspirators below and to save him from a charge of treachery. Four of the Jacobite conspirators were seized by the city guard,while the others ran into the unpunctual member of their party who was bringing the rope ladders, making his way beside the loch that was drained in a later age to accommodate the railway line to Waverley station.

The episode is somewhat typical of the fiasco of the 1715 uprising.

The castle's western defences were considerably strengthened in the 1730s, while the powder magazine on the summit above them was replaced a few years later by a tall ordnance storehouse, remodelled as a hospital in the nineteenth century. Such has been the process of transformation, new buildings replacing old or being superimposed upon them, to meet functional needs.

The most impressive that was erected between the 1715 and 1745 uprisings is the governor's residence, with its wings on either side to accommodate the storekeeper and the master gunner. It is of a simple, well-proportioned classical design, but with crow-stepped gables as a concession to the country's older vernacular architecture. Today the governor lives more modestly in a wing of this complex, while the central block has been transformed into the garrison officers' mess.

Over the Western Defences opposite its entrance that remarkable builder of military roads and bridges, Field Marshal George Wade, established a battery of six guns, which once looked down over open country to the Firth of Forth, where now the new town of Edinburgh stands.

General Guest was the castle governor when news arrived of the landing of Prince Charles Edward in the Hebrides, and General Sir John Cope was appointed commander-in-chief of the Hanoverian forces. He made a futile attempt to engage the Jacobites in the Highlands, and had not returned by the time Edinburgh opened its gates to Prince Charles on 17 September 1745. Charles took up residence in Holyroodhouse, while the two keys of the kingdom, the castles of Stirling and Edinburgh, remained in Hanoverian hands.

The Prince proposed to capture Edinburgh Castle as soon as he had defeated Cope at Prestonpans, and so this fortress was invested for the last time in its long history. When he ordered a strict blockade, General Guest sent word to the city magistrates that he would bombard their town as a reprisal. This resulted in a truce until some Jacobites in the houses below the esplanade fired on a party carrying provisions to the garrison. They were answered by a cannonade directed at these houses which lasted until the night on which soldiers from the castle made a sortie, set fire to some of the nearby houses, and dug a trench between the castle gate and the street below, where they mounted artillery. This persuaded the Prince to permit free communication between town and castle once more.

At the end of October he marched south into England and the siege was over. But even after Culloden, Edinburgh Castle continued to burgeon within its narrow confines. It was now that the ordnance store was placed on the very edge of the precipice and in front of it a row of carthouses, conveniently situated by the road that ran past the Governor's residence and through the old gateway to the palace square.

The largest single addition was to be the enormous barrack block built along the southern end of the rock after the outbreak of the Napoleonic war, between the Butts Battery and Dury's Battery. No such provision was made for all the French prisoners who were confined here. Earlier captives had been held in the vaults beneath the palace; now their numbers were enormously increased in those subterranean dens.

The prisoners left many mementoes of their presence here, some inscribed on the stonework. Among the objects they made for sale is the ship model, preserved in the United Services Museum, largely constructed of meat bones that they saved from their food. But their most profitable enterprise was the manufacture of counterfeit Scottish bank notes.

The nineteenth century witnessed a remarkable change in attitude to the castle. National pride, stirred by the pen of Sir Walter Scott, focussed upon it as the proud symbol of Scottish identity. People recalled that its battered palace had been for centuries the residence of kings of Scots. When George IV visited Edinburgh in 1822, he was the first reigning sovereign to set foot in the capital since the brief visit of Charles II in 1650. A procession was organized from Holyroodhouse to the castle, where the Lord Lyon and the Knight Marischal on their Arab steeds were not the least colourful of the assembled company. While some scoffed at all the fancy dress, and especially the riot of tartan, enthusiasm mounted to perilous heights among those determined to give the castle an appearance worthy of its history.

Ornamental walls had already been built on either side of the esplanade that leads to the entrance before George IV paid his visit. The new gatehouse, complete with the last drawbridge to be erected in Scotland, spanning the Cromwellian ditch, was not added until 1887. The statues of King Robert Bruce and Sir William Wallace on either side of it were placed in their niches as late as 1929. These additions have met with greater approval than the turret which was built above the palace block, previously heightened in preparation for James VI's visit in 1617. It was designed to carry the castle's flagstaff, which snapped during the great gale of 20 March 1986 but has since been replaced.

James IV's hall was restored through the munificence of William Nelson, the Edinburgh publisher. The partitions which had divided it into rooms for the accommodation of soldiers were removed. The hammer-beam roof was revealed, mercifully intact. Below it, a Victorian fireplace was installed, unsuited to these surroundings, and carved panelling to festoon the walls. On these have been hung claymores, while a miscellany of weapons and armour, brought from the Tower of London, is strewn around. However, the fabric has been saved, while Scotland's most precious souvenir in the Tower of London, Mons Meg, was brought home in 1822 and is preserved in an underground vault nearly as old as itself.

In the old palace the most interesting room is the one in which the royal regalia was walled up until it was reopened in the nineteenth century. The crown and sceptre of the United Kingdom on display in the Tower of London are more magnificent, but they are comparatively modern. Here are the oldest symbols of royalty to have survived in the British Isles: the crown refashioned by James V and believed to contain the gold from the circlet with which the Bruce was crowned; the sword of state sent to James IV by Pope Julius II in 1507; the ancient sceptre. Here too is James VI's bejewelled Order of the Garter, and the coronation ring made for Charles I in 1633.

The twentieth century has witnessed the apotheosis of the castle as the nation's shrine. It was still a barrack during the First World War, but people in the know were aware that this would not continue for much longer. In 1917, when victory was not in sight and casualties were mounting tragically, a proposal was launched that after the war a national memorial should be erected to commemorate those who had sacrificed their lives. There has been some controversy since as to who were the moving spirits supporting this project, and what were the parts they played. The unpublished diary of Sir Spencer Ewart, then General Officer Commanding in Scotland, describes the manner in which it took wing.

On 27 July 1917 he recorded: 'I gave a luncheon at the Caledonian Hotel to discuss my idea of converting Edinburgh Castle, after the War, into a National War Memorial and Museum. Among my guests were the Lord Provosts of Edinburgh and Glasgow, the Duke of Atholl, Lord Scott Dickson, Captain George Swinton, General Burney and Alastair Monro.' [The last of these was his son-in-law and father of Sir Hector Monro MP, the owner of his diary.] 'They all seemed impressed with my conception. I invited Lord Roseberry; but he could not come.' The eighth Duke of Atholl, whose father died in 1917, raised the regiment of Scottish Horse which he commanded in South Africa and at Gallipoli. It was he who had set the ball rolling when he sent a letter to the press suggesting that a National War Memorial should be built, and General Sir Spencer Ewart who proposed the castle as the most appropriate setting.

The Duke laid this project before King George V, as Ewart noted in his diary: 'On August 8th Atholl came to see me. He had been up to

London to have an audience with the King about my ideas as to the Castle War Memorial. Swinton came with him. His Majesty, he said, was very pleased with the notion, and a feature of the scheme now was that there should be an establishment of Scottish Yeomen of the Guard to take charge of the Memorial Building. It was hoped that each Scottish regiment would also have a room, in which to display their treasures, forming part of a General Naval and Military Museum.'

The memorial site chosen was that of the church of St Mary, which stood opposite the great hall of James IV. Here a barrack had been built in 1755 to replace the powder magazine constructed from the shell of the church. It was vacated in 1923 when the garrison was moved from the castle to Redford Barracks. The building, designed by Sir Robert Lorimer, contains the highest point of the rock, and here a casket containing the names of the dead stands in a shrine beyond the hall of honour in which all the Scottish regiments and every branch of the armed and nursing services are commemorated. Once work on the memorial building was completed, attention turned to that other project which had been mooted in 1917, the assembling of a United Services Museum. The task of collecting exhibits and displaying them in an appropriate setting has continued ever since, nor can it ever end so long as nations must continue to arm themselves for their defence.

In 1947 Edinburgh mounted its first International Festival of the Arts, and one of its entertainments was a Military Tattoo, staged on the esplanade below the castle. Since then this annual event has developed into perhaps the most spectacular that the Scottish capital has witnessed. Above it in the darkness the lighted walls of the half-moon battery incorporating the stones of King David's tower only half conceal the palace buildings behind. The effigies of King Robert Bruce and Sir William Wallace dominate the scene, guarding either side of the castle entrance.

STIRLING

Stirling Castle rises from its rock in the broad plain, framed by the surrounding hills. Below lies the River Forth at its highest navigable reach. The bridge that spanned it here was for centuries an important meeting place and junction, where passes converged from all the points of the compass in the heart of the kingdom. Beyond the Carse of Stirling to the west rise the Trossachs and Ben Lomond; equally far to the north the peaks of the central Highlands form a background to Strath Earn, while the nearer, lower Ochil range lies to the east and the Campsie Fells separate Stirling from the Clyde valley to the south.

On the summit of the Abbey Craig below the Ochils stands the memorial to Sir William Wallace. Within sight of the rock to the south-east, the equestrian statue of King Robert Bruce faces the field of Bannockburn. It was Robert Burns who placed in King Robert's mouth the incitement to battle that every school child learns to this day:

> *Scots, wha hae wi' Wallace bled,*
> *Scots, whom Bruce has often led,*
> *Welcome to your gory bed,*
> *Or to Victory.*

No fortress is more closely linked to the fortunes of these heroes, and consequently to those of the nation they preserved, than the one which rises from the rock of Stirling. It had ranked in importance with that of Edinburgh since the days of the Gododdin, and still did so when Edward I of England embarked on the subjugation of Scotland in 1296. By the time he reached Stirling, only a porter remained in residence to hand him the keys, but in the following year William Wallace and his compatriots arrived to do battle with the English Viceroy, the Earl of Surrey, as he prepared to cross the bridge with his army on his way to the castle.

This was long before the fifteenth-century stone bridge was erected here; the bridge which faced Surrey was made of timber. Neither did the castle from which the English garrison watched his approach resemble the one the visitor sees today. The old castle vanished long ago, and its appearance can only be guessed at.

13

On the morning of 11 September 1297 Surrey's cavalry began to cross the wooden bridge, two by two, and for several hours the Scots observed them, motionless. When the English army had been divided in two, a band of Scots demolition experts ran down to the bridge and set about its destruction, while the remainder rushed upon the English horsemen who had crossed the bridge and were now cut off. These were driven from the narrow causeway into the surrounding bogs, where their steeds floundered and threw their riders. The rest of the English army watched the massacre of their companions from the farther bank, unable to cross after the bridge had been breached. The Earl of Surrey fled, leaving his valuable baggage train behind. Those who sought safety in the castle did not find it for long.

Thus was the key to the kingdom restored to the Scots for nearly a year, before King Edward returned in person to defeat Wallace and recover it. When he reached Stirling Castle for the second time, he found it once again abandoned. Again the Scots recovered it after he was gone, which brought the Hammer of the Scots back for the last time in May 1304 with ingenious siege engines, and with lead that he had stripped from the roofs of Dunblane and St Andrews cathedrals and the abbey church of Dunfermline. This time there were defenders, who were driven by starvation to surrender unconditionally,

Ten years later the castle played its vital part in the greatest triumph of Scottish arms that had been seen in the nation's history. King Robert's brother Edward Bruce had entered into a pact with the castle's English commander that 'if by midsummer a year hence he was not rescued by battle, he would yield the castle freely'. Edward II arrived with his army on midsummer's eve 1314, and King Robert destroyed it on the field of Bannockburn. Stirling Castle was then dismantled, so that no souvenir of the war of independence remains on its rock. The earliest structures still to be seen here date from the reign of the Bruce's grandson Robert II, first of the Stewart kings. He succeeded in 1371, and ten years later the records refer to the North Gate. This provided a rear entrance by way of the lower platform at the north end of the rock, known as the Nether Bailey, and the modern road to it still passes beneath this arch.

As time passed, the Stewarts showed an increasing predilection for Stirling. Probably their earliest accommodation stood on the site of what is known as the King's Old Building, a complex so often reconstructed over the centuries that its original features are hard to discover. One room in it, however, is linked by tradition with James

II, who became king in 1437, when he was only six years old. It was he, aged ten, who witnessed the execution of the young sixth Earl of Douglas and his brother at the notorious Black Dinner in Edinburgh.

James II grew to manhood, the heir to his family's uneasy relations with the overmighty house of Douglas. In 1452 he invited the eighth Earl of Douglas to confer with him in Stirling Castle. Ominously, the Earl refused to come without a safe-conduct from the King. The pair dined before retiring to a small room for their talk, where James asked Douglas to demonstrate his loyalty by repudiating a private treaty he had made with the Lord of the Isles.

Douglas refused, and the two men fell to quarrelling. Finally, after exchanging verbal abuse, they resorted to their weapons. By the time the Captain of the Guard had entered with his men, alerted by the din, King James had struck the Earl in the throat with his dagger. The Captain despatched him with a pole-axe and it is said that his body was thrown into the garden below and there buried. The window from which it is thought to have been cast now contains a stained-glass window displaying the Douglas coat-of-arms. But the room which it lights is at the northern end of the old palace block, which was altered considerably after a fire in 1855. There is no real evidence that it was the scene of the Douglas murder in 1452.

But much else remains, both in castle and town, to make Stirling the most beautiful and evocative memorial to the cultured dynasty of Stewart. None of the buildings can be attributed to James II except a part of the structure of the church of the Holy Rood, for which he made a grant in 1456 'toward the building of the parish church of the burgh'. What additions his masons made is uncertain. The original church is older, while many of its finest features were added after his reign.

James III was born in the castle, and Robert Lindsay of Pitscottie the historian tells us that 'he took such pleasure to dwell there that he left all other castles and towns in Scotland, because he thought it most pleasantest dwelling there.' He founded the Chapel Royal in the castle, where he could listen to the choral music he enjoyed so much. It used to be assumed that his architect Robert Cochrane was the designer of the great hall that was built beside it, but now it is supposed that whatever James III may have begun here under Cochrane's direction, the work was completed in the reign of his son.

It was still being described as the architectural marvel of the age over a century later, after James VI had succeeded to the English throne and could compare the palaces of a richer and larger country with those of his native land. In 1618 an English visitor who inspected the building was moved to write: 'I dare affirm that his Majesty hath not such another hall to any house that he hath, neither in England or Scotland, except Westminster Hall, which is now no dwelling hall for a prince, being long metamorphosed into a house for the law and the profits.' John Taylor, a travelled man, declared that 'it surpasses all the halls for dwelling houses that I ever saw, for length, breadth, height and strength of building'. It is certainly superior to the hall that James IV built in the castle of Edinburgh, fine though that is.

But alas, it too was metamorphosed in a later age, and is only now being restored to its former glory. The task is being carried out with painstaking care and will take many years to complete, and in the meantime it is hard to visualise the sight that impressed John Taylor so deeply, amongst all the scaffolding and rubble.

It was built on a slope, like the hall at Edinburgh, and required a vaulted basement to give it a level platform. Its hammer-beam roof is of equal magnificence, while five large fireplaces are ranged along one of its walls to heat the enormous space within. On either side of the platform at one end, where the king would dine in state, there were two long windows in projecting bays, while the remainder of the hall was lit by pairs of smaller ones set high in the wall so that the stonework below could be brightened by decorative hangings.

The Royal Commission on the Ancient and Historical Monuments of Scotland, which is carrying out the work of restoration, has published its own description of the original features it has uncovered. 'Two spiral staircases at the north end gave access to a musicians' loft above the screened vestibule at the entrance, and to the walkway around the wallhead, whilst a third stair led to a balcony near the middle of the east wall, which overlooked the main body of the hall. There was also a fourth stair leading down to the basement, although this appears to have been blocked by the early eighteenth century, if not before.' The exterior, so elegant in its proportions, was seriously vandalised when windows and doors were inserted to serve the rooms into which the hall was divided when it was converted into a military barrack.

The stately new entrance that James IV gave to his castle can still be seen in a picture that was made in about 1680. He rebuilt the wall across the entire side of the rock that consists of a gentle slope, with rectangular towers at either end of it, a gatehouse in the middle with

semicircular towers on either side of the entrance, and other semi-
circular towers beyond them. All four were crowned with conical
caps. Today only the rectangular tower on the left remains: the
other was demolished to make space for an artillery platform. Of the
semicircular towers only those beside the entrance remain, their
height diminished, their caps gone, and nineteenth-century battlements added to them. Originally there was a portcullis of wrought
iron at either end of the entrance passage, each operated by a wind-
lass in the chamber above, and one of these still remains. So do the
dungeons whose only entry was a hole in the floor of the guard-
rooms in the gatehouse towers.

James IV's hall is a masterpiece of architecture whose style marks
the end of the Middle Ages. Beside it stands one of the earliest
triumphs of Renaissance classical architecture in the British Isles, the
palace that was built by James V. He was not so fortunate in his
mother as some of his predecessors had been. She was Margaret
Tudor, the sister of Henry VIII of England, quite the nastiest of
Scotland's queen consorts. But he married the best of them all, Mary
of Lorraine, and the French influence in the palace he built here must
be largely attributable to the masons she brought to the country.
Fortunately its marvellous exterior remains almost completely
undamaged, though some of the figures that decorate it have been
mutilated, notably St George who has been decapitated.

The palace surrounds a courtyard, its south face visible from the
esplanade below the castle; its galaxy of ornamental figures gazing
down over James IV's wall between the rectangular tower and the
gatehouse. Here the water-spouts represent boars, while a half-
naked woman, two entirely naked youths bearing shields and a splendid devil stand on the lower pedestals. On the smaller pedestals above
them, breaking the skyline, a bearded man holds his claymore, a
crossbowman winds up his bow, and two others brandish hand guns,
one firing his into the air.

On the east wall that faces the end of James IV's hall, the water-
spouts are disguised as winged creatures, while the ornate pedestals
support courtiers in their rich costumes. The detail on the north wall
can be examined more closely, because it faces the rising ground of the
upper square. Here the water-spouts are lions, and one of the figures
represents James V himself. The gargoyles and grotesques, the animals, humans, planetary gods and cherubs that look down from these
walls are a feast to the eye, a riot of the imagination. Here we witness

17

something very different from the mediaeval preoccupation with anointed kings and saintly people. There appears to have been only one saint here for a reformer to mutilate, if such was the fate of St George on the east wall. A more secular spirit had been at work here, bringing the exuberance of the Flemish Breughel, the German Burkmayer, the French masons who had worked on the magnificent chateaux of the Loire valley. Evidently the Scottish masons were caught by their enthusiasm, and worked alongside them with uninhibited delight.

The king's and queen's apartments occupied opposite sides of the palace square. The rooms have been cleared of the furnishings of the military garrison which occupied them until recently, and now stand empty, their great fireplaces hinting at their former magnificence. The fireplaces are decorated with some of the motifs to be seen on the outer walls: cherubs and birds, creatures half human, half animal, leaf ornament and thistles. Once the walls were hung with tapestries telling the stories of Troy, of Aeneas, Hercules and Coriolanus, as well as tales from the Bible. So the royal accounts testify.

But rarest of all, unique in fact, was the ceiling of the King's presence chamber, covered by a display of carved oak roundels that depicted all kinds of people from king to jester. It was still intact when John Macky described it in 1723, an observer as keen as John Taylor in the previous century, but more widely travelled for he was a secret agent who was sent on missions to the continent. He described this palace as 'the noblest I ever saw in Europe, both for height, length and breadth: and for the fineness of the carved work, in wainscot and on the ceiling, there's no apartment in Windsor or Hampton Court that comes near it. And in the roof of the presence chamber are carved the heads of the kings and queens of Scotland.'

A few decades later tragedy struck this ceiling. One of the roundels fell and injured a soldier beneath, and in 1777 they were all removed. Posterity owes a deep debt of gratitude to Ebenezer Brown, then governor of Stirling prison, who rescued many of the carvings from being burned as firewood. These became dispersed over the course of time, but twenty-eight of them have been recovered, and were restored to the palace in 1970. Three more are held by the National Museum of Antiquities in Edinburgh, two of which are believed to represent James V and Mary of Lorraine. The roundels have not been replaced on the ceiling for which they were designed originally, but are arranged on the walls of two rooms in the queen's apartments, where they can be examined more conveniently.

When Mary Queen of Scots returned home as the widowed Queen of France, she could not have found the palace of Holyroodhouse an impressive substitute for Fontainebleau. But there were Linlithgow, where she had been born, and Stirling, where she had been taken before she was a year old for her coronation. Here she could enjoy the favourite and most beautiful home that her family had created, worthy to be compared with any in France. She could see, too, how her family's standards of taste had influenced their subjects. During the reign of James V, John Coutts, a master mason of Stirling, had added a chancel and apse to the burgh church of the Holy Rude which stands as the last outstanding achievement of ecclesiastical architecture in Scotland before the Reformation.

The castle reached its apotheosis with the birth of the last Stewart sovereign to reign in his own country. James VI was born in Edinburgh Castle, but his mother brought him to Stirling for his baptism. Her marriage to the despicable Darnley had undermined her health and almost deprived her of her reason, but it had enabled her to achieve her dynastic ambition, the paramount goal of her life. Both of her son's parents were royal Stewarts, and in addition both shared the same Tudor grandmother, so that the offspring of their fatal union could not fail to inherit the English throne on the death of its barren Queen. Mary celebrated this triumph with a Catholic ceremony of unprecedented splendour in the chapel royal which James III had established in the castle of Stirling. The child's godparents included the King of France and Elizabeth of England, who sent a golden font.

After this, the increasingly erratic behaviour of the Queen of Scots soon led to her deposition, and within the year her son was crowned in her stead in Stirling's church of the Holy Rude, this time with Protestant rites.

King James was brought up in Stirling Castle, with Europe's outstanding Latinist George Buchanan as his principal tutor. The Earl of Mar, governor of the castle and Regent of Scotland, became his guardian. Immediately Mar built himself a mansion below the esplanade, decorated with gargoyles, masks and heraldic panels as though in emulation of the royal palace. But he died soon after its completion and today only its ruined façade remains, above the main street of the burgh.

There was repeated strife between rival groups jockeying for power until James was old enough to begin his personal reign, and the castle was fortunate to sustain no damage as each of them attempted to obtain possession of the source of authority, the young King's person. James might well have grown to hate this place in which, instead of parental love, he endured the chastisement and relentless instruction of Buchanan, the periodical perils and alarms. Yet he seems, on the contrary, to have retained an affection for his childhood home, and it was here that he chose to have his son and heir baptised as he had been himself.

Whatever the condition of James III's chapel by the time Prince Henry was born in 1594, his father had it rebuilt in some haste before the ceremony. It was given a classical entrance in the form of a triumphal arch, with three pairs of windows along the walls on either hand. Early in the following century its rather severe interior was enlivened with flower designs on the roof timbers and heraldic devices on the upper walls.

Prince Henry's baptism was a sumptuous affair as his father's had been, attended by representatives of Denmark, his mother's country, and other European states, while the child was carried by the Earl of Sussex on behalf of Queen Elizabeth of England. Suspended from the roof above their heads was a wooden crown and iron models of the castles of Stirling, Edinburgh, Dunbarton and Blackness. Tapestries hung from the walls, and the pulpit was draped with cloth of gold. The ceremony was followed by a feast in the great hall that must have rivalled any seen there before.

Even the guests from the sumptuous court of Christian IV of Denmark must have been impressed. A Blackamoor entered, drawing a chariot laden with all kinds of fruit and confectionery. No sooner had he departed than a trumpet heralded the appearance of a boat, fourteen feet in length, containing fifteen musicians with hautboys, flutes, violins and a harp, who made music while a cargo of sweetmeats in the shapes of fish were unloaded in crystal glasses. The ship's masts were painted red, its sails were white, the cordage of silk and the pulleys of gold, while the anchors were tipped with silver.

Prince Henry spent the first nine years of his life in Scotland, and grew up intelligent, devout, conscientious, universally admired. It was a disaster when he died at the age of eighteen, leaving his younger brother Charles as heir to the two kingdoms. King Charles spent only two nights in Stirling Castle, on his visit to Scotland in 1633, and his quarrel with his subjects heralded the downfall of his family's most beautiful home.

After his execution, his son Charles II was crowned and paid a brief visit in 1650. But he was defeated by Cromwell, and in the following year General Monk arrived in command of the army of the Commonwealth and laid siege to the royalist garrison. He bombarded the castle for three days before, fortunately for its fabric, a mutiny within compelled its commander to surrender. Monk carried away the palace hangings as well as forty pieces of ordnance, leaving a force of men to hold the fortress. Two years after he himself had stage-managed the restoration of Charles II in 1660, there were still two hundred English soldiers in occupation of the ghost-palace of the Stewarts.

But although the Stewarts were gone forever, their royal burgh continued to enjoy an Indian summer throughout the seventeenth century. The Earls of Mar remained in the office of hereditary governor of the castle, and lived in state in the mansion overlooking the commercial centre surrounding the mercat cross. Other courtiers of a vanished court still added their stimulus to the activities of life here, notably Sir William Alexander of Menstrie.

Alexander was a pioneer of colonisation, who obtained in 1621 a royal charter for the colony to be called Nova Scotia, and published his *Encouragement to Colonies* four years later. He became Secretary for Scotland soon after the accession of Charles I, who created him Earl of Stirling and also bestowed on him the bizarre title of Viscount Canada. Below the castle esplanade he built himself a fine house that was purchased after his death by the Earl of Argyll, and is known today as Argyll's lodging. William Alexander dissipated his wealth in many directions and died heavily in debt, but much of it must have found its way into the pockets of his fellow citizens in Stirling.

While such noble patronage continued long after royal patronage was withdrawn, local enterprise also flourished through the long established commerce with foreign countries. Prominent among its success stories is that of John Cowane, at one time head of the Guild of Merchants in Stirling, who traded with Holland in the ships that could sail up the River Forth as far as here, but no further. Cowane bequeathed an endowment with which to build a retirement home for elderly merchants, and work started on it in 1634, at a time when the Earl of Stirling's town house was being erected. It stands near the church of the Holy Rude, and a statue of Cowane in an alcove of the bell tower displays the dress worn by such men in that age.

In the nearby cemetery can be seen the souvenirs of another order of people whose lives were enriched by aristocrats and merchants, and who enriched Stirling in their turn. On the gravestones are chiselled the glove and cutter of the skinners, the scissors and iron of the tailors, the shuttle and thread of the weavers, the knife and hatchet of the fleshers. Other symbols commemorate the shoe-makers, hammermen and agricultural workers. Seventeenth-century prosperity is attested also by the substantial house that James Norrie the Town Clerk built for himself in 1671, which still stands on the Broad Street, between the mercat cross and the ruin of Mar's mansion.

The eighteenth century brought changes. French ships appeared in the Firth of Forth in 1708, with the Old Pretender on board, and although he returned to France without landing, immediate steps were taken to improve the defences of Edinburgh and Stirling castles. In both cases it was Captain Theodore Dury the Royal Engineer who planned and supervised the work, which confronts visitors as soon as they approach the castle.

A massive curtain wall rises beyond the drawbridge and the ditch it spans. In the thickness of the ramparts are vaulted chambers for the accommodation of soldiers while above them batteries were mounted. One of these is called the Queen Anne battery, named after the sovereign who was occupying the throne claimed by her brother the Old Pretender. Her cipher appears on the keystone of the inner gateway that was added between the drawbridge entrance and the old gatehouse of James IV. Behind it lie what are now known as the Queen Anne Gardens. The emergency for which these formidable additions to the fortress provided occurred soon after their comple-tion. Queen Anne died in 1714, and in the following year the Earl of Mar raised the Jacobite standard, challenging the succession of George I from Hanover.

Immediately the Hanoverians occupied the castle in defiance of its hereditary governor, and their commander-in-chief in Scotland, the Duke of Argyll, came to their support. By holding the vital crossing of the Forth, still spanned by its fifteenth-century bridge, they contained the Jacobite army in the disaffected north. A thousand and a half of its braver members crossed lower down in boats, to face defeat in England, while that incompetent grandee the Earl of Mar remained

Edinburgh Castle

The Great Hall in Edinburgh Castle

Stirling Castle

Left The Douglas Window in Stirling Castle; *above* The Palace, built by James V between 1538 and 1542; *below* The Chapel Royal, with painted decoration by Valentine Jenkins

Left Blair Castle; *above* Niel Gow by Sir Henry Raeburn; *below* 3rd Duke of Atholl and family by Johann Zoffany

The Drawing Room in Blair Ca

The Dining Room chimney-pie

inactive until Argyll came to meet him at Sheriffmuir in the pass north of Stirling, with an army a third the size of his own. Although Mar did not quite suffer a defeat, his movement crumbled until he fled the country.

What might have been the fate of Stirling's palace if he had won is an interesting speculation. The Earl of Mar possessed his family's interest in architecture, and occupied himself during his exile in designing a building more in keeping with the taste of the age. His blueprint reveals how little would have remained of all those exuberant decorations of the age of James V. But the Earl died over a decade before the Young Pretender arrived in 1745 to revive his father's claim to the throne, and once again the Jacobite cause was lost.

But not before the castle and its precious buildings were gravely menaced for the last time. The town surrendered to Prince Charles, but General Blakeney in the castle rejected his ultimatum when he arrived at Bannockburn in January 1746, on his return from England. The Prince laid siege to the castle, but his guns were not well sited nor his dispositions competently planned. His army suffered severe losses without any compensating gain before it retreated north.

So the last opportunity to restore a Stewart court in Stirling vanished, and its palace, like that of Edinburgh, was gradually defaced in the course of its transformation into army barracks. James VI's chapel suffered the fate of James IV's hall in Edinburgh when it was divided into two floors, and partitioned to serve the needs of garrison troops. The subterranean kitchens in which banquets had been prepared were filled in to provide a firm foundation for an artillery platform.

The great gateway into the town known as Barras Yett, at which tolls were charged on goods entering and leaving, was demolished in the eighteenth century. Much of the wall it pierced, that had encircled the burgh in a loop from either side of the castle rock, has disappeared. But a long stretch of sixteenth century construction remains.

Old town houses that were still standing when the present century opened have been demolished since then. But the church of the Holy Rude is among the precious survivors from pre-Reformation Scotland. Cowane's hospital is intact, and Argyll's mansion, and the seventeenth-century dwelling known as Darnley house. The elegant tollbooth designed by Sir William Bruce and completed in 1705 stands beside the courthouse and jail that were added a century later.

The old bridge was still a vital artery in 1835, as Johnstone remarked: 'There cannot, upon some occasions, be fewer than from thirty to forty thousand head of cattle, and nearly fifty thousand sheep, which all pass this one bridge.' It no longer possesses the guard houses between the central arches, nor the gateways at either end. But this five-centuries-old link between north and south still spans the Forth below the rock, though now it is barred to traffic.

So although there has been loss, much remains to excite wonder and delight. The enthusiasm for conservation now embraces this ancient royal seat. After the Second World War the chapel royal was restored to its original state, except that no church furnishings were replaced in it. Instead it serves as the memorial hall of the regiment of Argyll and Sutherland Highlanders, with a roll of honour on the wall at one end. In the old palace buildings beside it in the upper square is housed the regimental museum.

The mediaeval kitchens beneath their artillery battery have been excavated and reconstructed. When the Great Hall of James IV which they served has been restored, the jewel of Stirling Castle will stand once more as a fitting memorial to the brave and accomplished King who perished on the field of Flodden in 1513.

BLAIR

Far beyond the mountain peaks visible from the Carse of Stirling, a far smaller plain lies at a junction of passes in the central Highlands. Here Glen Tilt and Glen Garry converge on Blair Atholl from north and west, while in the south Strath Tummel is separated from it by the pass of Killiecrankie. In this strategic centre stands Blair Castle, white-harled and crowned by crow-step gabled towers, conical corner turrets and battlements framed by the surrounding trees. This is a nineteenth-century reconstruction, encapsulating earlier buildings that have dominated the region for over seven hundred years.

Once this was the heartland of the kingdom of the Picts, and legend tells that it was bestowed by the Pictish King Cruithne on his son Fotla. Hence its name Fotla's Ford, *Ath Fotla*, or Atholl. After Kenneth Mac Alpin had set himself up as King of the Picts and Scots in 843, Atholl became one of the earldoms of the royal house of Alpin until the male line died out in the thirteenth century. The castle belonged to the royal domain when King Robert Bruce died in 1329, and was involved in the second war of independence during the reign of his son David II. Mercifully this was shorter than the first one, but Edward III of England stayed at Blair Castle in 1336 during his expedition through the Highlands. At that time it may have consisted of no more than the keep built by John Comyn during the previous century. It has been much altered since, but is still commemorated as Cumming's Tower, in the north-west corner of the present structure.

Most curiously, it was a descendant of Edward III who became earl of Atholl just over a hundred years after the English King's visit, precisely by virtue of his Plantaganet blood. It happened like this. James I, King of Scots, was taken prisoner by the English in 1406, and in London he fell in love with Joan Beaufort, Edward III's great-grand-daughter. She came to Scotland as his queen and was still relatively young when he was murdered by his relatives in 1437. She made a second marriage with Sir John Stewart, known as the Knight of Lorne, a person of little consequence. It was not because their son was a Stewart, but because his mother was a Plantaganet, that his step-brother King James II made him Earl of Atholl in 1457.

The third Stewart Earl lived until 1542, by which time he had built a wing from the mediaeval keep known as Cumming's Tower, extending to another tower to the south of it. The great hall it contained was transformed in a later age, but not the vaults which supported it on their stone arches between walls of massive width. Here may be seen the portraits of James V, who also died in 1542, and of his wife Queen Mary of Lorraine. There is a miniature of their daughter Mary Queen of Scots, who attended a hunt here in which 360 red deer were killed. Here is displayed the justiciary sword, symbol of the authority which the earls wielded in their sovereign's name.

Another portrait depicts Mary Queen of Scots and her son James VI. It was during his reign that the fifth earl died in 1596, leaving a daughter Dorothea as his heiress. Her miniature is preserved in the same cabinet as that of her queen. Lady Dorothea Stewart married William Murray, second Earl of Tullibardine, whose likeness we can also see in the vaults, together with that of their son the first Murray Earl of Atholl. The Murrays have lived in Blair Castle from his time to the present.

By passing from one vault to the next, we leave the sixteenth century, to encounter the people and events of the seventeenth. The great quarrel between Charles I and his subjects originated in his attempt to introduce a high church liturgy in Scotland, and one of the four copies of the National Covenant of protest that was drawn up in 1638 is displayed here. The Earl of Atholl supported the King, and the leader of the Covenanters, Campbell of Argyll, consequently imprisoned him in Stirling Castle in 1640. Two years later he died, to be succeeded by his eleven-year-old son John Murray as the second Earl. He was too young to share in the brief triumph of the royalists under the gallant Montrose, barely of age when the troops of Cromwell came to occupy his castle after the defeat of Charles II in 1651. But his portrait keeps company with that of Montrose in the same vault that holds the National Covenant. There is even a four-poster bed of the same period here.

In the adjoining guardroom are grimmer souvenirs of those days of violence, instruments of restraint and torture from the prison that lay beneath. The bones of three men were discovered in the nineteenth century, buried in the vicinity. They are believed to have been victims of the second Earl's attempt to recover possession of his castle in 1654.

He came into his own at the Restoration of 1660, and to take the short step from those low vaults to the grand staircase beyond is to pass into the very different world which the Murrays of Blair Castle helped to create in the century that followed. On its wall hangs the great portrait of the second Earl by Jacob de Wett, dressed as a latter-day Julius Caesar except for his full-bottomed wig, pointing with his baton to the Battle of Bothwell Brig in the background. Here he helped to suppress the Faithful Remnant of the Covenanters in 1679. He had been created Marquess of Atholl three years earlier, and in 1680 he was appointed Vice-Admiral of Scotland.

His family's good fortune might have been short-lived if he had remained loyal to the Stewart dynasty when James VII was dethroned by William of Orange in the revolution of 1688. But providentially he had married a descendant of the earlier William of Orange, liberator of the Netherlands, and it can hardly be doubted that it was his wife who influenced him when he transferred his allegiance.

Her name was Amelia Stanley and she was a daughter of the Earl of Derby. Her portrait is framed on the wall above the great stairway to the left of her husband's. Lower down the stair is a picture of her mother Charlotte de la Trémouille, dressed severely in black and white, the descendant of the house of Orange. During the civil war her home, Latham House in England, had been besieged by the opponents of Charles I, while she sat with her needle, embroidering the bed hangings which may still be seen in Blair Castle. The episode is described in Walter Scott's novel, *Peveril of the Peak*.

The choice between James VII and his mother-in-law's kinsman in 1688 placed the Marquess of Atholl in a dilemma. He solved it by travelling to take the waters at Bath, while his heir joined the Williamites and his younger son remained at the castle to welcome the Jacobites commanded by Viscount Dundee. In July 1689 John Murray the heir arrived with his Orangemen to lay siege to his own home. There followed the battle in the pass of Killiecrankie a few miles to the south, in which Dundee was fatally wounded in the hour of victory.

He was carried back to the castle, where he died, and the Jacobite cause expired with him. The helmet and breastplate of John Graham, Viscount Dundee hang in the castle vaults, near to the portrait of that earlier hero of his clan, James Graham, Marquess of Montrose. The Marquess of Atholl lived prosperously into the reign of Queen Anne. When John Murray his son succeeded as the second Marquess in 1703 the Queen raised him to a dukedom.

But although Queen Anne gave birth to a succession of children, none of them lived. The question of the day was whether she should be followed on the throne by her brother in exile, James Stewart the Old Pretender, or by her nearest Protestant relative, George of Hanover. Once again a Murray of Atholl was faced by a choice between the house of Stewart and a rival to whom he was related, for the Hanoverian claim derived from the Winter Queen of Bohemia, daughter of James VI, whose son Prince Rupert had fought so gallantly for Charles I but left no heirs, so that the claim passed through one of his sisters. All of these people were cousins of the Earl of Derby's daughter, Amelia, Marchioness of Atholl. Nor are they mere names, lost in the footnotes of history. In the tea-room at Blair Castle hang stately portraits of them by that most fashionable Dutch artist, Gerard van Honthorst: Elizabeth of Bohemia, her son Rupert of the Rhine, and all the sisters except for Sophia who was the mother of George I.

However, the Duke of Atholl did not support the succession of his cousin when he was proclaimed King in 1714. He was dismissed from the offices he had held in the reign of Queen Anne, of Keeper of the Privy Seal and High Commissioner. His sons did worse. William, Marquess of Tullibardine, his heir, proclaimed the Old Pretender as King James VIII at Dunkeld, supported by his brothers Lord Charles and Lord George Murray. When the Jacobite uprising of 1715 failed, Tullibardine and George Murray fled abroad while Charles was taken prisoner. Although their father the Duke had stood aside, he was gravely compromised.

But he survived. On the castle stairway his portrait depicts him, pointing towards his mansion at Dunkeld, whatever that was intended to signify. And while his heir the Marquess of Tullibardine lived in exile, a disinherited Jacobite, his younger son James succeeded as the second Duke at his death in 1724.

Twelve years after he had become the master of Blair through the exclusion of his elder brother, he found himself heir to a second bonanza. The Derby family to which his grandmother Amelia belonged were sovereigns of the Isle of Man. Now, through a dynastic accident, this inheritance of the Stanleys passed to the house of Atholl. The Duke celebrated his good fortune by embarking on an extensive transformation of his home, from a mediaeval castle into a Georgian mansion. Fortunately there are water-colour sketches made in 1736, which preserve its appearance both from the front and the rear before these massive alterations to the building were begun.

Duke James was also the first to introduce larch trees from the Tyrol, which were to transform the surroundings of the castle in the years to come. He had by no means completed his improvements when Prince Charles Edward landed in Scotland in July 1745, accompanied by the Duke's elder brother, the Marquess of Tullibardine. In September they moved into Blair Castle, abandoned by Duke James. As soon as they were gone a Hanoverian garrison was installed, and so it was that Blair is the last castle in the British Isles to have undergone a siege, one in which brother fought against brother for the ducal coronet of Atholl as well as the British crown. It was conducted by the Duke's younger brother Lord George Murray.

After remaining a fugitive abroad in the aftermath of the 1715 uprising, Lord George had returned home in the year of his father's death. He obtained a pardon and leased the family property of Tullibardine in Strathearn from his brother. It was not until Prince Charles moved into Blair Castle in September that he decided to risk his fortune once more in the Stewart cause, and he soon proved himself the ablest of the Jacobite commanders. On 21 September he defeated the Hanoverians at the battle of Prestonpans.

But neither Prince Charles nor his closest advisers quite trusted this late-comer to their cause. The Chevalier Johnstone was to write that 'had Prince Charles slept during the whole of the expedition, and allowed Lord George Murray to act for him according to his own judgment, he would have found the crown of Great Britain on his head when he awoke.' Lord George opposed the march into England, recommended the retreat from Derby, and was largely responsible for the army's safe return to Scotland. There he won the final Jacobite victory at Falkirk and laid siege to his family castle. Red hot shot fell on the roof of the old tower, and a segment of the damaged woodwork has been mounted in the entrance hall as a souvenir. But here, as at Stirling, the siege failed.

After the defeat of Culloden Lord George escaped to the continent again, where he was received gratefully by the Old Pretender in Rome, but snubbed by Prince Charles in Paris, who blamed him for the failure of his attempt. While he lived in exile in Holland, consoling himself with his library of books, his brother the Duke celebrated the Hanoverian victory with a trophy of arms that was designed for the space above the fireplace of his new dining room. A full length portrait of this fortunate man dominates the upper landing of the grand staircase that he completed in 1756, with elaborate plaster-work on ceiling and walls.

The tale of conflict between him and his brother Lord George Murray has a delightful ending. Duke James possessed only two daughters, the elder of whom died in 1747. Her younger sister Charlotte then became heiress to the sovereignty of Man and the barony of Strange, while Lord George Murray's son John was heir to the dukedom. In 1753 the cousins married, the two branches of the family were reconciled, and its property preserved intact. Lord George in his exile lived to witness this match, though he died four years before his son succeeded as the third Duke of Atholl in 1764, and became proprietor of the castle his father had bombarded two decades earlier.

The new Duke and Duchess resigned their sovereignty of Man to the government in 1765, for the sum of £70,000. But they retained their very considerable property rights in the island. These were sold to the Crown in 1828 for £417,000, a sum equivalent to millions at the present value of money. In the Derby room of the castle there are portraits of Charlotte, both as a young girl with her sister, and as the Duchess. This is where the embroideries of Charlotte de la Tré-mouille are also to be seen, while in the adjoining rooms are pictures of the Isle of Man, and specimens of the coinage which the Atholl family issued there in the time of their sovereignty.

The son of Lord George Murray was able to bring souvenirs of a very different kind to Blair Castle. In one of its oldest rooms, known as the Tullibardine room, hangs the famous portrait of his father as a Jacobite commander, dressed in the kilt and carrying his weapons. Another more conventional likeness depicts him in civilian dress, wearing a wig. Beside it stands a tent bed with tartan hangings about two hundred years old. Here too hang a drawing and a painting of Prince Charles, and pictures of his parents, his mother the Polish Princess Clementina Sobieska, and his father James, the Old Pretender.

Downstairs in the treasure room other Jacobite souvenirs are displayed: samples of the tartan worn by the Prince, documents, miniatures and the small personal possessions that people gave one another as mementoes. It is curious to find a building in which relics of both the protagonists in a conflict that divided one of the most powerful families in the land are gathered under the same roof.

In the great drawing room, with its walls of crimson damask and its richly plastered ceiling, hangs a portrait by Zoffany of the third Duke, his cousin-wife and seven of their eleven children. They are seen by the water's edge, trees around them and mountains in the background, framed in baroque elegance above the marble chimneypiece. Their eldest daughter Charlotte, depicted holding a wreath of flowers, was to embroider all the covers of the twelve chairs and two settees in the drawing room. In this she was following the estimable example of her step-grandmother Jean Drummond, who had worked the covers of the eight chairs in the smaller drawing room, and may well have given the girl personal instruction during her old age.

Standing beside his father in Zoffany's painting is the young heir, who was to become known as 'the planting Duke' after he had succeeded to the property. While his sister Charlotte appears to have been influenced by the Dowager Duchess, he responded to that of her husband his grandfather, whom he had known as a child. Following his example, he planted the larch tree on a larger scale than had ever been seen in Scotland.

The drawing room contains cabinets made of local larch wood, covered by tops of marble quarried in Glen Tilt. A full-length portrait of the fourth Duke hangs above one of these, and there is an expressive bust of him, fashioned by the Perthshire sculptor Lawrence MacDonald, in an alcove at the end of the room, thoughtful in his old age. He had been Lord Lieutenant of Perthshire for over thirty-five years, and raised the local militia during the Napoleonic war. But this did not distract him from publishing his *Observations on Larch* in 1810.

For a century after John and Charlotte succeeded to the dukedom in 1764, their very home reflected the transformation of the family's style of living. It was not a castle any more, though it had so recently withstood a siege as such. The fourth Duke had himself painted as a young man with his family, just as his father had done, his mansion in the background among its well ordered parklands. No towers, battlements or corner turrets disturbed its symmetry. On the other hand, the Duke did choose to have himself depicted in the kilt, the proscribed costume of the Gael, in a picture by David Allan.

In the ballroom of the castle hangs a portrait by Sir Henry Raeburn of Niel Gow. This most celebrated of Scotland's fiddlers was born in 1727 a short distance from Dunkeld, and in the year of the Forty-Five, before he was out of his teens, he won a fiddle competition open to every performer in Scotland. It was not long before he had also earned himself a reputation as a composer for the instrument. He became musician to the second, third and fourth Dukes. In 1972 Sir Yehudi Menuhin paid tribute to his memory by playing Gow's tribute on the death of his second wife before his portrait in the castle.

This region had always been a cross-roads, at which many of Scotland's diverse cultural traditions met. The great Gaelic bard Duncan Bàn Macintyre also belonged to Perthshire, and he was Niel Gow's almost exact contemporary. David Stewart of Garth recalled listening to Duncan Bàn, whose immortal songs undoubtedly enlivened the same occasions as Niel's fiddle did. The dukes of Atholl emerge in a new light as the artistic patrons of this time and place.

In 1787 Robert Burns arrived from the Lowlands, and was entertained hospitably by the fourth Duke, a young man only four years the bard's senior. At Blair Castle he was introduced to the Laird of Fintray, Robert Graham, who was to secure his appointment and his promotion as an officer of the Excise. Burns's poem in honour of the visit could not have had a more tactful theme. It was a humble petition from the stream called Bruar Water, begging the Duke to plant trees along its banks. The prayer was granted, and this is one of the most beautiful local sights to be seen in Blair Atholl today.

> *Here, foaming down the skelvy* rocks,*
> *In twisting strength I rin;*
> *There, high my boiling torrent smokes,*
> *Wild-roaring o'er a linn†:*
> *Enjoying large each spring and well*
> *As Nature gave them me,*
> *I am, altho' I say't mysel,*
> *Worth gaun a mile to see.*

> *Would then my noble master please*
> *To grant my highest wishes,*
> *He'll shade my banks wi' towering trees,*
> *And bonie spreading bushes.*
> *Delighted doubly then, my Lord,*
> *You'll wander on my banks,*
> *And listen mony a grateful bird*
> *Return you tuneful thanks.*

* shelfy † waterfall

The fourth Duke died in 1830, in the same year as George IV. It was left to his descendants to give expression to the romantic mediaevalism of the age, inspired by the writings of Sir Walter Scott.

One of the most extraordinary manifestations of this enthusiasm was the Eglinton Tournament, held at the castle of Archibald Montgomerie, thirteenth Earl of Eglinton, in 1839. It was said to have cost him upwards of £40,000, something approaching a million pounds at today's value of the currency. It was a genuine joust in which spears were broken by the charging knights, as in the Middle Ages; with a Queen of Beauty, later to become the twelfth Duchess of Somerset. The Emperor Napoleon III took part and it was altogether a very grand affair, though it was marred by a ceaseless deluge of rain and excited a great deal of ridicule.

The Atholl heir had a suit of armour made for the occasion, and horse trappings, lance and banner. He made an appearance at Eglinton unlike any other for he was the only British subject who was permitted to maintain his own armed bodyguard, like the sovereign. They were, and still are, known as the Atholl Highlanders, and he arrived with an escort of seventy of these, accompanied by four pipers. His accountrements for the tournament are still preserved in the castle, mounted on a dummy horse at the foot of the second staircase, on which the sixth Duke appears to sit, his lance at rest. A painting was made of him, standing on foot in his armour, and beside it another of his Atholl Highlanders as they appeared on parade in 1842. They were armed with halberds. It was not until later that Queen Victoria gave them permission to bear firearms, and presented the Colours which hang in the dining room except when they are borne on ceremonial occasions. The Duke struck a medal to commemorate the charade of Eglinton, and issued it to every member of his private army who attended. It is not the least bizarre memento on display in the castle.

For a castle it became once more during the reign of his son the seventh Duke. The work of rehabilitation was carried out between 1869 and 1872 to the designs of David Bryce, one of the most talented exponents of the Scots Baronial revival during the nineteenth century. It is arguable that Blair Castle is his greatest masterpiece, not least because of the difficulty of the task he set himself here. While so many others simply vandalised the work of earlier ages in order to achieve the effect they desired, Bryce succeeded in preserving the classical interiors of the Georgian era intact, while he restored the external appearance of a castle that had been altered and enlarged over the centuries and had served originally as a fortress. The tower was refashioned, and high above the surrounding roofs the banner of Atholl still flies today when the Duke is in residence, depicting the heraldic bars of black and gold.

A great hall was added by Bryce, such as the nobility used in the Middle Ages, though today it serves as a ballroom. Instead of gutting the interior to restore its original great hall, he designed a low wing beyond the castle complex, with a passage of larch wood about a hundred yards long. The only baronial addition which Bryce incorporated into the main building was his grand entrance hall, complete with old weaponry and a stuffed stag.

Its impressive proportions have, of necessity, been marred by the offices that were required here when the castle was opened to the public. The sixth Duke on his horse, apparelled for the Eglinton Tournament, no longer dominates the entrance but skulks under the stairs, his lance menacing nobody except those who are collecting the entrance fees from visitors.

In the ballroom hangs a portrait of his grandson the eighth Duke, whose dress proclaims a very different sort of military record. It is the uniform of the regiment of Scottish Horse that he personally raised in Atholl and commanded with conspicuous gallantry, first in the Nile expedition of 1898, then in South Africa from 1899 until 1902, and a decade later at Gallipoli. He represented West Perthshire in Parliament during the First World War, until he succeeded to the dukedom on his father's death in 1917. But this did not detain him from active service, until he reached the rank of Brigadier in 1918. It was he who first conceived the idea of a Scottish National War Memorial.

The eighth Duke married perhaps the most remarkable of all the Atholl wives. Katherine Ramsay was the daughter of a tenth Baronet of that name from Banff, who was a brilliant classical scholar. Katherine herself became the outstanding classical scholar of her year at Girton College, Cambridge. In 1923 she became the first woman to be returned to Parliament by a Scottish constituency, and in the following year the first to be appointed to ministerial office. Appropriately, she served in the Ministry of Education, until the Conservative government fell in 1929 and Ramsay MacDonald took office as Prime Minister.

The Duchess continued to sit in the House of Commons until 1938, supporting causes that earned her the epithet 'The Red Duchess'. She associated with those remarkable Members of Parliament of very different political affiliations, Eleanor Rathbone and Ellen Wilkinson, waging war on the cruel practice of female circumcision, and organising help for the Republican refugees during Franco's war in Spain. She supported Winston Churchill in the wilderness during the era of appeasement.

Portraits and a bust in the castle commemorate this little squirrel of a woman who possessed such a brilliant intellect, such a humane heart and such independence of mind. She was a strange partner for the martial Duke. Perhaps it was she who influenced him to open their home to the public in 1936, when this was a much more eccentric step than it would be today. During the Second World War the castle was closed to the public while it was used as a military hospital, and during the conflict her husband died. Since the pair were childless, he was succeeded by his brother.

The ninth Duke had served in South Africa with the eighth, as a Cameron Highlander. He had been wounded and taken prisoner in 1914, which helped to ensure his survival, but he died unmarried in 1957. A remote cousin, Sir George Murray, was his heir presumptive, but he died in 1947, two years after his son, who was killed in action, commanding the Scottish horse that his kinsman had founded. Thus it was Sir George's grandson who became tenth Duke and current owner of Blair. Remote collateral as he is to the senior line of Atholl, he can see his ancestor in the Zoffany portrait of the third Duke and his cousin-wife, a little boy without expectations standing in the corner behind his mother.

The Duke of Atholl presides over some of the most valuable public amenities provided by any Scottish castle in private ownership. By June 1986 over three million people had visited it since it was opened to the public fifty years earlier in 1936. There is a caravan park in the castle grounds, the old water mill is kept in working order, and there is also a museum of Atholl life. The Duke himself is a vice-president of the National Trust for Scotland and honorary president of the Scottish Wildlife Trust. He keeps his home in a wing of the castle and his eye on its activities. Only when he wears his regalia to inspect his private army of Atholl Highlanders is he conspicuous among the crowds who throng the castle and grounds of Blair.

INVERARAY

Argyll is roughly of the dimensions of the kingdom of Dalriada, set up by the *Scotti* from Ireland in the fifth century. Its long waterways run south-west towards the land from which the original Scots came, bringing their Gaelic language with them. East of the Mull of Kintyre Loch Fyne penetrates inland for seventy miles from the open sea before it reaches the castle of Inveraray, and there are about ten miles more to the head of the loch.

Whether the Campbells who built the successive castles of Inveraray in the heart of Argyll belonged to the Scottish kinship groups of Dalriada remains in doubt. There were centuries of conflict between the Campbells and neighbouring clans who undoubtedly did so, MacDonalds and MacDougalls, MacGregors and Macleans. While all of these take their names from a historical ancestor, the Campbells alone among Highland clans possess a mythical one. In Gaelic they are known as Clan Diarmaid of the Boar, in supposed descent from the Ossianic hero, while Campbell is a descriptive term, *Cuim Beul*, Crooked Mouth. It may be that the Campbells were aboriginal inhabitants of British, or even Pictish stock, menaced by the colonizing Scots, whose language they adopted with its folk legends.

They prevailed over all their rivals. Innischonnaill Castle on its island in Loch Awe was their headquarters in mediaeval times. Sir Colin Campbell of Loch Awe married a grand-daughter of the first Stewart sovereign Robert II, and the chiefs of his name have been addressed ever since as *Mac Cailein Mór*, Great Son of Colin. His grandson received the earldom of Argyll in 1457, and it was he who built himself the high L-shaped tower at Inveraray on the banks of Loch Fyne. In 1472 a burgh of barony was established in its vicinity, and in 1648 this was erected into a Royal Burgh by a charter which decreed that it should be the sole market and fair in the sheriffdom of Argyll.

The eighth Earl and only Marquess of Argyll, to whom this privilege was granted, was the devout leader of the Presbyterian Covenanters in their rebellion against Charles I. As a result, he was executed after the restoration of Charles II in 1660. His son, inheriting his religious opinions, was executed in his turn, while his grandson fled into exile to escape a similar fate. He returned with William of Orange in the revolution of 1688, the final triumph of the Calvinist Reformation in Scotland which his family had been the first of their rank to support, and to which they had remained faithful ever since, in good times and bad.

The Earl of Argyll was created a Duke, and the people of Inveraray might have expected to share in his prosperity. But the Duke was busy in the southern world of politics, while his son had embarked on a brilliant military career. In those days the journey to Inveraray was long and arduous, situated as it was in a mountainous country without roads. In 1709 the inhabitants of the burgh sent a petition in which they described their extreme poverty, the ruinous state of the harbour and streets, the lack of any public works. Of their proprietors they complained: 'the said noble family have not had so frequently their residence in this place'.

During the Jacobite uprising of 1715 Inveraray was besieged and the tolbooth damaged. The insurrection was suppressed largely through the skill of the second Duke of Argyll, the commander-in-chief in Scotland. He rebuilt the tolbooth, repaired the church and erected two schools and a bridge. But by now the old castle was in a dangerous state of disrepair. The walls bulged and wind whistled through their cracks. The Duke built himself another tower beside it but not connected to it, which came to be known as 'the pavilion'.

The disincentive to further improvement was that the martial Duke possessed only daughters who could not inherit, while his heir was a widowed brother, Archibald, who likewise possessed no legitimate son. Yet it was this brother who transformed Inveraray when he succeeded to the dukedom in his sixty-second year.

Allan Ramsay's portrait of him in the new castle he built depicts him in more flattering terms than others used. Lord Hervey, who was his political colleague, wrote of his 'mean aspect', while Horace Walpole described him as 'slovenly in person, mysterious, not to say with an air of guilt, in his deportment'. He haunted bookshops, assembling the finest private library in the country, cared little for social rank, and managed his country's affairs so skilfully that he became known as 'King of Scotland'.

His brilliant, versatile mind had already turned to agricultural improvement before the problems of Inveraray became his responsibility. Born in Ham House near Richmond, he transformed the waste land of Whitton on Hounslow Heath into a nursery for trees and shrubs, many of them imported from abroad, and made a canal there. In Peeblesshire he reclaimed a barren moor, where William Adam built him a house. In the month of his brother the second Duke's death he wrote: 'I am thinking of getting some sort of manufacture to Inveraray.' He had not set eyes on the place for nearly thirty years, yet he wrote in November 1743, 'I intend if possible to remove the town of Inveraray about half a mile lower down the loch.'

Duke Archibald set out from London in July 1744 and it took him five weeks to reach his family seat on Loch Fyne. In his entourage he brought Roger Morris, an architect of Welsh descent who had designed a number of Palladian houses in England. It was arranged that Morris should meet William Adam on his return south through Edinburgh. Adam possessed four sons, still in their youth, two of whom were to become known as the Adam Brothers. The third Duke had determined that he would rescue the capital of the Campbells from the decades of neglect, and he set about it with his characteristic efficiency. He brought to the task his flair for choosing able and dependable men, whom he treated as colleagues rather than servants. A Member of Parliament remarked: 'The ducal coronet is not the least bar upon him and he goes about and does everything as usual.' A clergyman observed that, 'He never harangued or was tedious, but listened to you in your turn.'

When the Duke Archibald reached Inveraray in 1744 the castle was ruinous beyond repair, but he was able to live in the pavilion beside it that his brother had built. Nearby, the most substantial houses of the burgh surrounded their mercat cross, and the new bridge spanned the Aray river near the town centre, from which the church steeple rose. Thatched houses extended towards the river mouth and the loch. Although the Duke had determined in advance that he would remove the burgh to a better site, he made no move to demolish the old one before alternative accommodation was ready. Neither did he pull down the old castle, although he had decided to build a new one. He simply planted this in the space between the old burgh and the crumbling tower house.

But it appears that he arrived with his ultimate intentions already formulated. At the height of the current fashion for classical architecture, he employed two masters of the Palladian style, Morris and William Adam, to initiate a return to the gothic, baronial kind of castle. At the same time, he set the earliest example of systematic town planning to be seen in Scotland. That two such different conceptions as the turretted castle and the town of classical design should have been given shape in one place in the 1740s is remarkable enough. That a locality at the time so wild and innaccessible as Inveraray should have been selected is the crowning wonder.

It was Roger Morris who designed the castle, a sort of toy fort on a huge scale, a tour de force as eccentric in its day as the man who commissioned it. The castle is rectangular, with a circular tower at each corner almost detached from the central block, and one floor higher. But these in turn are dominated by a three-fold central tower. The effect was somewhat diminished when the corner towers were given tall conical caps in the nineteenth century. Originally they had flat roofs behind their castellated battlements. A dry ditch, nine feet deep and thirty-five feet wide, reproduces the curve of the corner towers as it encircles the building. It is crossed by gothic bridges to north and south.

While there is nothing quite like the exterior of this castle, Roger Morris displayed equal originality within. The central hall rises to a ceiling in the central tower, seventy feet in height, with staircases on either side of it, all lit by enormous gothic clerestory windows. Morris had paid a preliminary visit to Inveraray before he completed his plans, and he and Duke Archibald explored the site before the first excavations began, in pouring rain. After their departure, William Adam would arrive to supervise the work.

Adam determined to use stone from the nearby Creggans quarry, which is of a blue-grey colour that turns almost black in rain. 'There is full proof of its being durable,' he noted, 'as many stones of the old castle are from that quarry.' However, as work progressed, other stone was brought from the St Catherine's quarry on the opposite side of the loch. This is of a greenish-brown colour and it was used in the central tower, whose appearance contrasts with that of the corner towers around it.

A road was to be built through the rugged mountainous country between Dunbarton and Inveraray. Since 1725 Field Marshal Wade had been penetrating the Highlands with his military roads, and this was to be one of them. Engineers carried out a survey in the summer of 1744, and early in the following year soldiers of the 23rd Regiment began work at the Dunbarton end. By the time it was completed, the troops had built no less than eighteen bridges as they advanced over the difficult terrain between the head of Loch Long and the head of

Loch Fyne. Roger Morris's beautiful bridge over the Garron river awaited them as they moved along the shore towards Inveraray. With its balustrades and ornamental stone balls on the parapets, spanning the tidal water, it provides an enchanting foreground to the sights beyond.

Work on both castle and road was interrupted by the Jacobite uprising of 1745. The Duke was detained in the south by affairs of state, but his first cousin and heir, General John Campbell of Mamore, came with his regiment of the Scots Fusiliers to garrison Inveraray. The General's son Colonel Jack Campbell was there before him, raising and drilling a militia. Even after the defeat of the Jacobites at Culloden in April 1746 the Duke had to remain in London for the treason trials. He was crippled by attacks of rheumatism and migraine, but remarked that he kept going with 'the help of a terrible deal of pills'.

However, there was William Adam to supervise the building of the castle while Morris and the Duke were otherwise engaged, and he reached Inveraray to do so in September 1746. General Campbell, who would become the fourth Duke on the death of a man already elderly and infirm, presumed to suggest alterations to Adam, and was rebuked by Duke Archibald as soon as he learned what was afoot. By December, Adam was able to report that 'the foundations of the house with the common sewer have been carried on as fast as the nature of the season would admit and in everything agreeable to Mr Morris's plan and directions.'

The exact part which William Adam played here is clearer than, for instance, in the case of Floors castle.

But Adam was called away by other commitments, and by the time he returned in 1747 he had to report shoddy workmanship in the absence of proper supervision, as well as embezzlement of materials. But now at last Duke Archibald was able to return, and in August there occurred the first meeting on the spot of the three men who were creating this castle between them, Roger Morris, William Adam and the Duke. It was also the last. Adam died of a kidney disease in June 1748, while Morris fell ill at the same time and expired in the following February. It says much for the indomitable spirit of Duke Archibald, who was older than either, that he brought their work to completion without them.

Adam's responsibilities were taken over by his eldest son John, while henceforth the Duke visited Inveraray annually until 1760, the year before his death. His directing hand was seen everywhere, and the Chamberlain of Argyll, Archibald Campbell of Stonefield, remarked significantly that his presence 'makes everybody about him happy'.

He laid out the parks and woodlands. Returning to an earlier ambition of his, he established an industry in the old town while the new was still under construction. In 1751 Mrs Elizabeth Campbell started teaching local girls to spin. Two years later 'the spinning business is now so successful that there's 112 wheels kept going by females, besides three more occupied these ten days by boys.'

Duke Archibald lived to see the structure of his castle completed, wedged between the old burgh and the tower ruin. But its interior was not ready for him to move in by the time he died in 1761. In his late seventies, he might have expected that. But in the last decade of his life he did see others occupying the houses of the new town that was his greatest gift to Scotland.

Placed on its headland half a mile from the old site, it was built according to plans designed in the first instance by William Adam, and modified by his son John and by the Duke himself. The final version contained a central square in which the church was to constitute the focal point of the burgh, facing east with a main street running down to the shore. Parallel to this there was to be a long avenue, with an inn beside its entrance. Along the waterfront beyond the inn should stand a courthouse and the homes of burgesses. Unlike the castle, all these buildings were to be classical in design.

The inn was designed by John Adam in 1750 and opened in 1755, and although some alterations have been made to it since, the original conception is not seriously altered. It was John Adam also who was responsible for the new courthouse, its three storeys surmounted by a pediment. Originally its central portion projected over arches open to a piazza which led to the prison within. The courtroom was above, and a schoolroom on the top floor. The piazza has been closed in since, but the houses forming lower wings on either side remain much as they were when the complex was completed in 1757.

The earliest houses built within the specifications laid down for the new town were the homes of the prosperous burgesses. John Richardson, a merchant who later became Provost, completed his at Fern Point in 1753, and in the same year two more were added on the waterfront, one for Baillie Peter Campbell the wigmaker, the other for Provost Alexander Duncanson. The round church designed by

William Adam for the central square seems to have been lost among his papers at his death, and the space it should have occupied was still empty at Duke's Archibald's death. But the church in the old burgh was there to serve.

Dukes came and went, but no duchess had been seen in Inveraray for as long as anyone could remember. Duke Archibald's wife had died long before he inherited, and the cousin who was to succeed him was already a widower also. Consequently it was an especial delight to Duke Archibald when Jack Campbell, the heir after his father the General, married in 1759. At the age of thirty-five he was promoted Major-General like his father, in that very year, and in the autumn he brought his bride to view the castle of which she would be one day the first chatelaine.

Elizabeth Gunning was one of those rare women about whom nobody could find an ill word to say, despite her rise from a penniless background and her enviable beauty. She was the widow of the Duke of Hamilton, and continued to use his name, as the mother of the young Duke, until she became the fifth Duchess of Argyll ten years later. Of her portraits in the castle, one must arrest every visitor. In it she wears no jewellery and does not appear to have used a hairdresser. There was no need.

On his last visit in 1760 Duke Archibald saw his new castle still standing cheek by jowl between the church spire of the old town and the L-shaped tower, and a painting attributed to John Clerk preserves the sight. Evidently demolition did not appear so important to him as construction. A gothic dairy was being added to the amenities during his last years, new stables were under construction, and an office block. The Duke had permitted himself the extravagance of 'a folly' on the summit of Duniquaich from which he had first viewed his property as a Duke in 1744, a watch-tower with a rough rubble surface that was completed in 1752.

What remained incomplete had to wait for a decade after General Campbell succeeded as the fourth Duke, until he was followed in 1771 by Jack Campbell and his beautiful wife. Now the castle became a true family home at last, and the era of its embellishment began.

The presiding genius was Robert Mylne. His celebrity is so much slighter than that of the Adam brothers that it is startling to recall how he won a prize in Rome, at the age of twenty-five, under the jealous eyes of Robert Adam. Mylne's younger brother William was studying with him in Rome at the time, and it was he who made the first alteration to the castle, reversing the two fronts so that its main entrance was at the opposite side. But from 1772 it was Robert Mylne who performed such outstanding services to the Argyll family for the next thirty years.

His are the sumptuous decorations of the castle's public rooms. In designing these classical interiors, Mylne was faced by the problem that the windows possessed gothic pointed arches, and that their alteration would damage the external appearance of the building. The task of preserving the pointed arches on the outside while giving the rooms windows with rounded arches, seen from within, took years to complete.

Then work began on these rooms according to Mylne's detailed specifications. The saloon, the largest of them, was walled with silk and hung with family portraits. As for the dining room, this has been described as the finest in the entire house, and here every surface of wall and ceiling is adorned with designs in paint, plaster-work and gilding with an artistry that helps us to understand why Robert Mylne had been awarded his prize in Rome. The glass above the fireplace is framed subtly with painted feathers and leaves. Over the doors the sensual pleasures of food and drink, warmth and scent are depicted in relief.

The drawing room was designed to frame a set of seven Beauvais tapestries on its walls. Floral panels enclose the glass above the mantelpiece and in the high space above the doors oil paintings of the ruins of antiquity are framed. Much of the furniture of these rooms was acquired by the Duke and Duchess while the work was in progress, Hepplewhite chairs covered with Aubusson tapestry, Beauvais tapestry suites, exquisitely carved and gilded. Work on the interior of the castle lasted until about 1789.

But the man whose brave military career had brought him to the rank of General when he was thirty-five years old did not decline into a dilittante after succeeding as the fifth Duke. He reached the rank of Field Marshal, and every year he made an inspection of Scottish fortifications and troops. In addition, he inherited the third Duke's concern for the economic improvement of the Highlands. He became the first President of the Highland and Agricultural Society, and when the British Fisheries Society was founded in 1786 he immediately espoused its objectives. In that very year he adopted the advice that Tobermory in Mull was a suitable site for a fishing port, and so this charming little town came into existence at the same time as Mylne's decorations.

His concern for the modernisation of agriculture bore fruit in yet another building at Inveraray that was new to Scotland. In 1771 he made an inspection of the local farm lands which concentrated his mind on the problem of saving crops from the hazard of a wet season. Mylne was instructed to design barns in such a way 'that there may be a free passage for wind and air to dry the corn.' The building technique they devised between them included latticed apertures which excluded rain but admitted air to circulate round the sheaves hung on pegs along the walls.

It was employed in the magnificent complex of buildings at Malt-land, near the castle. Here a smith's forge, coach houses and stables, in addition to the great barn, surrounded a gravelled courtyard. 'The magnificent drying barns of the Duke of Argyll, so far famed, and the only ones of the kind in Scotland,' were widely admired and studied minutely by other agriculturists. Mylne designed another for Glen Shira, and this time he made it circular with an ingenuity derived from his previous experience. But this one was only half completed. Its semi-circular structure is still there to admire, together with his working drawings for the whole.

While the focal point of the new town still remained without its church, it became urgently necessary to provide some form of prem-ises for public worship there after the succession of the fifth Duke, because one of his first steps was to demolish the old town under the windows of the castle. Mylne's new church was not completed until 1800, and during the interval the English and Gaelic congregations met in the two halves of what is now the George Hotel.

Mylne's church was his last service to the Duke, and caused the quarrel between them that terminated their long and fruitful associa-tion. It was designed to contain the English and Gaelic churches back to back, the exterior giving no hint of its dual function. Both the English artist Turner and the Scottish Nasmyth made paintings of it during its construction.

The Duke had a more serious quarrel on his hands than his differ-ences with Mylne. His heir the Marquess of Lorne had become one of the most dissipated rakes of London society, until his astronomical debts threatened to bankrupt the estate. His father begged him to mend his ways, and save him 'from being plunged into despair by your misconduct'. But his extravagances continued, until Lady Louise

Stuart predicted that 'there will be an end of this fine place'.

The son of the lovely Elizabeth Gunning was something of an Adonis. 'He is very handsome, well-made, and like a gentleman.' So Lady Holland described him, but added, 'He has in his disposition an uncommon share of indifference, almost to apathy, and though in possession of every requisite for happiness, it does not appear that he enjoys anything.' His consolations for this misfortune were gambling and women.

From 1806 when he succeeded as the sixth Duke, until 1839 when he died, the estate and its buildings reflected increasingly the effects of insolvency and neglect. Woods and parklands deteriorated, Mylne's plasterwork decayed in the great rooms of the castle. But the Duke's younger brother Lord John did what he could to remedy the situation. When a typhus epidemic broke out in 1818 he set up a fever hospital to tend the victims. He joined the Fisheries Board and the town authorities in paying for an extension to the pier.

The old court-house, with cells for prisoners on the ground floor beneath it, was proving inadequate. Lord John acted as chairman of the comission which planned its replacement, a role that the indolent Duke ought to have filled. By 1820 James Gillespie's handsome new building had been completed. Its Georgian front faces the town square, while behind it the walls of the jail rise above Loch Fyne.

Lord John had good reason to do what he could to preserve the property, because he was the presumptive heir to it. His elder brother possessed no legitimate children, though plenty of bastard ones. In the end, Lord John was given eight years in which to continue saving his inheritance from ruin, in the more advantageous position of seventh Duke. He was then followed by his twenty-four-year-old son, already married to the daughter of the fabulously wealthy Duke of Sutherland. The menaced castle survived the squalor of its Regency era, and the Victorian age found it a scene of cultivated and happy domesticity.

In 1847 Queen Victoria herself sailed up the loch to visit the young Duke and his wife, with Albert and their small children. One of these, Princess Louise, was later to marry the Duke's heir. Her portrait still looks down on a room that reflects the taste of her time, so different from that of the previous century.

Early on the morning of 12 October 1877 a fire broke out, which seriously damaged the centre of the castle, destroying the roof of the main tower and the woodwork of the hall. An architectural journal reported: 'The whole of the valuable decorations of the hall have been destroyed . . . The tapestries in the principal drawing-room are much injured by having been hurriedly torn down when that part of the building seemed in immediate danger.'

The temptation to transform Inveraray castle according to the fashion of the Victorian age had received an unlucky stimulus. The Duke commissioned Anthony Salvin, a leading designer in the romantic baronial style, to carry out the restorations, and in the circumstances the result might have been much worse. But an additional storey was added and those conical caps placed on the corner towers, so that the central one lost its commanding height. The private drawing-room and the state bedroom, now the private dining room, received ornate plaster ceilings.

Mercifully, Mylne's decorations had survived the conflagration, and the tapestries could be repaired and restored to their places on the walls of the great drawing-room.

The eighth Duke was a Liberal statesman, who served under Gladstone. He was also a prolific author. But his most memorable service to his country was to have given such enthusiastic assistance to his cousin John Francis Campbell of Islay, the father of Gaelic folk-lore studies. As a result, the castle library contains a manuscript collection of Gaelic oral tradition such as no other Highland Chief possesses.

The Duke's son, the Marquess of Lorne, became Governor General of Canada before succeeding his father in 1900. Unhappily he and his wife the Princess Louise were childless, so that the title passed after his death in 1914 to a succession of nephews.

The first of these, Duke Niall, made a disastrous addition to the architecture of Inveraray. The eighth Duke had built a little gothic Episcopalian church behind the town, which was not in the least intrusive. After the First World War the tenth Duke added a campanile, or detached bell tower, which soars above the burgh, an utterly discordant element in the general design. When the steeple of Mylne's church, the original focal point of the burgh's skyline, was taken down in 1941 because it was considered unsafe, the grotesque campanile was left without a rival.

Duke Niall died in 1949, unmarried. By this time the castle grounds had been used as an army camp during the Second World War and were littered with its debris. The houses of the town were in a state of disrepair and lacked modern sanitation. The castle required more expensive renovation than the Argyll Trustees could well afford when Duke Niall's cousin became the eleventh Duke. The Historic Buildings Council and the Scottish Development Department came to the rescue with grants, the burgh properties were transferred to the custody of the Ministry of Works, and by 1963 the delightful town of Inveraray had been rescued.

The castle too was repaired, but after the succession of the twelfth Duke it was threatened with destruction once again in November 1975. A small fire broke out in a linen cupboard, and spread throughout the upper floors until the entire roof burst into flames. The damage was such as no insurance policy could have made good, but the Duke was determined that the seat of the Campbell chiefs should be saved and his clansmen throughout the world rallied to the cause. Their devotion to the preservation of this national treasure was well rewarded. Some valuable paintings were lost in the fire, but the tapestries and the Mylne plaster-work were saved, and the staterooms are now to be seen once more as he created them.

So it is that the thousands of visitors to Inveraray can still inspect those two strange and wonderful adornments of Loch Fyne, the gothic castle and the classical burgh, more or less as the third Duke of Argyll conceived them over two hundred years ago. In the castle offices they can also see an exhibition of the military activities which enlivened this neighbourhood during the Second World War. The most enlivening of today's activities are the Highland Games that are held in July, when Mac Cailein Mór leads the march through the town to the castle policies for an explosion of piping, dancing and athletic events.

CULZEAN

The waters of Loch Fyne are divided on their journey south by the Isle of Arran. To the west of its cliffs they flow down Kilbrannan Sound past the coast of Kintyre. To the east they enter the Firth of Clyde as it makes its way past Ayrshire. On a high cliff about midway between Ayr and Girvan stands the castle of Culzean, with its view on a clear day of Kintyre and the mountains of Arran, and those that hide Loch Fyne in the farthest distance. Culzean is one of the most spectacular masterpieces of the architect Robert Adam. Whatever disappointment he suffered when his rival Robert Mylne was commissioned to work at Inveraray, he was amply compensated when he was invited to transform this castle.

The building he found here was very different from the one the visitor sees today. Originally it had consisted merely of a mediaeval keep with a single room on each floor, all connected by a winding staircase in a projecting tower. This had been demolished late in the seventeenth century, and replaced by a more commodious dwelling. Adam himself is thought to have made the sketch of it from the south, showing the high tower complex with its gabled roofs and barmkin wall.

There were ancillary buildings that contained a brewhouse and laundry, milkhouse and stables. The minister of nearby Maybole wrote in 1693 of 'pretty gardens and orchards, adorned with excellent terraces, and with the walls laden with peaches, apricots, cherries and other fruits'. Perhaps these were still well-tended when Robert Adam made his first improvement plan in 1777. Certainly there was a plain, functional building on the edge of the cliff, between the castle and the sea. This was the home of a sept of the Kennedy clan whose chiefs, Earls of Cassellis, lived a few miles away in the castle of Cassellis by Doon Water. It was a mere dynastic accident that made Culzean the seat of the senior line of the Kennedys for a while. But that happy accident gave Robert Adam the opportunity which inspired him to such heights of invention.

Culzean had played little part in the long history of the Kennedys until comparatively recent times. It stood in the ancient Celtic earldom of Carrick, and it has been surmised that the Kennedys belonged to the house of Carrick, which descended from the royal house of Galloway. In Turnberry Castle, a few miles down the coast from Culzean, the future King Robert Bruce was born to the Countess of Carrick in her own right in 1274. A lighthouse stands on its site today, and only a few fragments of its crumbling walls remain.

Far to the south, there was a Kennedy castle near Stranraer during King Robert's reign. But the ancestors of the lords of Culzean were living in the castle of Dunure, round the headland to the north of Adam's castle, in the time of David II, as a charter of 1345 reveals. Today it is also a ruin, though a more substantial one than Turnberry. Sir James Kennedy of Dunure married the Princess Mary, daughter of the second Stewart King Robert III, and the eldest son of this union was created Lord Kennedy sometime before 1458.

By this time the family had acquired their property a short distance inland up the valley of the Doon, where they built their new home, the castle of Cassellis. They were soon erecting others as they proliferated throughout the south-west. The first Lord Kennedy possessed five brothers, including Sir John of Carrick, Thomas the founder of the branch of Bargany south of Turnberry, and James the reforming Bishop of St Andrews who became Chancellor of Scotland in 1444. So powerful did the clan become that the saying went:

> *Twixt Wigtown and the town of Ayr,*
> *Portpatrick and the Cruives of Cree,*
> *No man need think to bide there*
> *Unless he court with Kennedy.*

The third Lord Kennedy had been raised to the earldom of Cassellis by James IV before he perished with his king on the field of Flodden in 1513. His promotion in the peerage may not have been unconnected with the fact that his sister Janet was one of the mistresses of that amiable sovereign. Gilbert the third Earl married his cousin Margaret, daughter of Alexander Kennedy of Bargany, a not uncommon practice designed to preserve property within the kinship group. As a result, their younger son Sir Thomas of Culzean descended from both branches.

A portrait of Sir Thomas hangs in the castle, painted in 1592 when he was forty-three years old. He wears the tall, wide-brimmed hat of the period and the eyes beneath are shrewd. When the fourth Earl died in 1576 through a fall from his horse, Sir Thomas administered the estate of Cassellis as tutor to the dead Earl's eight-year-old son. This involved him in a family vendetta which cost him his life.

It originated in a scramble for the abbey lands of Crossraguel. When Alan Stewart accepted the office of abbot, the fourth Earl imprisoned him in the black vault of Dunure and roasted him over a slow fire until he signed away his church properties. But in 1570 Abbot Stewart was rescued by Thomas Kennedy of Bargany, and then repudiated his signature. After the fifth Earl had grown to manhood he waylaid Gilbert Kennedy of Bargany and his following of eighty men with a party of two hundred, and slaughtered them all. The outrage occurred near Maybole in 1601.

Sir Thomas of Culzean was believed to have been responsible, and he was butchered on the sands of Ayr by Bargany's brother in a revenge killing in 1602. The Bargany murderers were executed, while the fifth Earl was never called to account. Indeed, he was promoted to the office of Lord Treasurer of Scotland. But he failed to produce an heir and was succeeded by a nephew on his death in 1615.

During the seventeenth century wars of the Covenant, Sir Archibald Kennedy of Culzean became known as 'the Wicked' in pious circles, because he was among those who persecuted the Faithful Remnant of the Covenanters. It comforted some of these to believe that the devil attended Sir Archibald's funeral and that his corpse was carried off to hell by friends in a fiery chariot.

His cousin the seventh Earl earned himself an equally bizarre reputation. It is preserved in legend, and also in the portrait of his first wife which hangs in Culzean today although she herself probably never entered the castle. She was Jean Hamilton, daughter of the Earl of Haddington, a victim of one of those arranged marriages to which girls of her station were expected to submit without demur. Folklore relates that she was in love with another man, and was not consoled by the rank of Countess of Cassellis.

> *Gae tak' frae me this gay mantle,*
> *And bring to me a plaidie,*
> *For if kith and kin and a' had sworn,*
> *I'll follow the gypsie laddie!*

The painting in Culzean depicts her wearing the finery she was prepared to toss aside for the embraces of Johnny Faa, the gypsy king of the ballad. It tells that he came to rescue her from Cassellis with a party of men. But they were caught by the banks of the Doon and all killed except for Johnny Faa and the Countess. These were brought back to the castle, where she was compelled to watch from a window while he was hanged from the dule tree beneath its walls. She was then confined in the Earl's prison in Maybole until she died, still a young woman, in 1642. Such a romantic tale has survived the protests that it is untrue.

The Kennedys escaped every pitfall of the rebellion against Charles I and the revolution of 1688, and it was during this period that Culzean was rebuilt in the form that Robert Adam saw. Sir Thomas Kennedy inherited Culzean in 1744, and so far from being among the casualties of the Jacobite uprising which followed, he found himself heir to the earldom of Cassellis fifteen years later, when the eighth Earl died without sons. His right was contested by a Douglas, claiming through female descent, but in 1762 the House of Lords decided in his favour.

The ninth Earl was a lifelong bachelor, so was the brother who was his heir. It is all the more astonishing that neither of them should have elected to move out of their comparatively modest castle into that of Cassellis, but devoted their lives instead to transforming the castle and improving the estate of Culzean, merely to pass both on their deaths to a remote relative who lived abroad. In taking this course, both men revealed the enthusiasm of the artist who is driven by a demon within to create something for its own sake.

Thomas, ninth Earl of Cassellis was less interested in the elegance of his family seat than in agricultural improvement. He merely added the plain block of buildings on the cliff in front of his castle, and others to serve the needs of the home farm. From 1758 he began the enclosure of his lands with dykes and hedges which defined larger farms and involved the removal of the smaller tenants. Stones were removed from the fields, which were levelled by ploughing, drained and manured. The rotation of crops was introduced, and green crops for the winter feeding of cattle.

Bulls were brought from a distance to improve the black Galloway breed. The number of sheep was sensibly diminished, while an improved strain of horses was bred. As late as 1752 all goods were still carried by pack horses, and no wheeled vehicles were used. Gradually this was remedied as roads were built. The planting of trees also played its part in the metamorphosis of the surroundings of Culzean, until they lost their unkempt appearance and wore the mantle of good husbandry that the visitor sees today.

The brothers lived in close partnership, though their portraits hang in different rooms at Culzean. They went on the grand tour of Europe together in the 1760s, where Thomas was esteemed for his manners and his musical skill. His younger brother was evidently spellbound by the renaissance architecture of Italy, and it was here that he was painted by Batoni, as so many other Scottish aristocrats were at this time.

They attended parliament together, the Earl as a representative peer, his brother David in the Commons. James Boswell scoffed in his journal that 'the gentlemen of Ayrshire should be represented in Parliament by a good, honest, merry fellow indeed, but one so incapable of the business of legislation, and so devoid of the talents which distinguish a man in public life'. David was to belie that judgment after he had succeeded his brother as the tenth Earl in 1775.

Almost at once he approached Robert Adam with an invitation to improve the amenities of his castle. This was carried out in successive stages, beginning with the very modest proposals of 1777. One of the most remarkable aspects of what Adam achieved is that he preserved so much of what was there already, and that he devised new additions with such skill that the final result might appear to have been conceived as a whole from the start.

First, the seventeenth-century house was enlarged by rooms that were added on either side, creating a symmetrical front in the Georgian manner. But while its large windows were of classical design, they were surrounded by corner turrets containing crosslet windows and crowned with battlements, echoes of a past age and harbingers of the gothic revival to come. The work began in 1777, and by the time it was completed a visitor reported: 'His Lordship, not content with the present extensive pile, intends adding a similar front to the sea, which will be a most arduous undertaking from the vast depth of the foundation necessary to be formed.'

It involved the demolition of the ninth Earl's modest block on the cliff edge, and of other out-buildings that were removed in 1785. In their place rose the great round tower that holds Adam's circular saloon.

Two years later, Adam conceived his final masterpiece. Between the drum tower and the castle behind it there was a courtyard in its dark well. This he filled with the oval staircase that connects the two. Light pours from its glass dome, down the three storeys to the foot of the staircase. From below, the perspective is influenced by Adam's use of the more elaborate Corinthian columns on the first floor, and of the shorter, plainer Ionic ones on the floor above, reversing the traditional order. The central stair divides on an intermediate landing, from where the mahogany handrail curves with the stairs in a parabola on either hand to the landing which leads to the saloon. They ascend no further. The floor above, with its Ionic columns surrounding the balcony, is reached by another staircase.

Within the building, Adam attended to the minutest details. Like the tenth Earl, he had made a close study of the renaissance arts of Italy, which he recreated here, starting in the ground floor room of the seventeenth-century tower, now encased in additions of his own. Today it is furnished as a drawing room, but he decorated it as a dining room, with a frieze of vine leaves and grapes that he also placed above the doors and on the marble mantelpiece. Roundels in the ceiling, here as elsewhere, were painted by the Italian Antonio Zucchi, husband of the equally famous artist Angelica Kauffmann. In this room John McClure from Ayr began to carry out, to Adam's specifications, the exquisite plasterwork that he extended to so many other ceilings in the castle.

Above the fireplace was a mirror of Adam's design, and on the walls elaborate candle brackets called girandoles, which incorporated little round paintings as well as swans, the supporters of the Kennedy coat-of-arms. Ceilings, girandoles, friezes, mirrors were likewise designed for other rooms, with infinite variety and ingenuity.

None is more impressive than the grand saloon. Here a carpet, incorporating the swan motif, was woven locally in shades of colour that matched those of the plasterwork of the ceiling above. On the walls, delicate oval chairs stood beneath the hanging girandoles. Through windows that extended to the floor between them was a sight that contrasted dramatically with this palatial interior. The stone balustrade on a narrow balcony hung over a 150-foot cliff, with a view beyond of the sea breaking on this rugged coast, of the mountains of Arran across the water, of the Firth of Clyde extending northwards to the peaks that surround Loch Fyne in Argyll. The confrontation of art with nature achieves an effect that none who have witnessed it will ever forget.

In what had been the high hall of the old tower house hang outstanding paintings by Alexander Nasmyth, which display Robert Adam's completed work, from the south and from the sea, before Victorian alterations were made. Between them is Batoni's portrait

Top Inveraray Castle; *left* 3rd Duke of Argyll by Allan Ramsay; *right* Elizabeth Gunning by Catherine Read

The Dining Room in
Inveraray Castle

The Armoury Hall

The Tapestry Drawing Room

Above View of Culzean Castle from the north-east by Alexander Nasmyth; *below*
The Castle today

The Oval Staircase

The Saloon, recently restored to Robert Adams' original design

Above Glamis Castle
Below The Sundial
Right The Chapel

Above 3rd Earl of Strathmore and Kinghorne with his sons and hunting dogs
Below The Drawing Room

of the tenth Earl, in yet another room adorned with its own special Zucchi paintings and friezes, plasterwork ceiling and mirrors, candle brackets and chimneypiece. Both the architect and his patron died in 1792, leaving all these wonderful things to Captain Archibald Kennedy, Royal Navy, who was settled in New Jersey. He did not enjoy his inheritance for long, for he died in 1794, but at least he left a son to take his place as the twelfth Earl of Cassellis.

The son of the Sailor Earl formed a friendship with the Sailor King, who created him a Marquess in 1831, the year after he ascended the throne as William IV. The twelfth Earl took his new title from Ailsa Craig, the rock that rears its head out of the Firth of Clyde so dramatically some miles south of Culzean.

The third Marquess of Ailsa succeeded at the age of twenty-two when his father was killed in a hunting accident, and he lived to the age of ninety. It was he who built the new west wing in the 1870s, matching the castle's earlier architecture. This helped to save Adam's interiors from more alterations than they sustained in the event. But an outer entrance hall was added to the original one, which was enlarged by removing the wall that divided it from the buffet room. Today a magnificent display of weaponry decorates these walls, swords and pistols and bayonets that were issued by the twelfth Earl to the West Lowland Fencible Regiment, raised to meet the threat of invasion by Napoleon.

Robert Adam's dining room with the frieze of vine leaves and grapes was lined with oak book cases and converted into a library. Victorian wallpaper was placed on the walls of the picture room in which Nasmyth's paintings of Culzean hang today. The different metals used in ornamental supports of the balustrades in the oval staircase were concealed under a coating of gilt paint. The subtle colours of the saloon ceiling became lost under a coating of white. In the drawing room which Adam designed in the 1780s, a gasolier was suspended from the centre of a Zucchi painting. The proportions of a charming little barrel-vaulted ante-room were spoiled by the installation of a lift. It might have been much worse but for the wing added by the third Marquess when he inherited the property in 1870.

His long reign was the apotheosis of the home and estate that had been created for him by the bachelor brothers a century earlier. Among the new amenities was a railway that ran along the coast from Turnberry through the grounds of Culzean to Dunure. Only a single section of it is still to be seen on the edge of the park, a bridge spanning its cutting. Despite this novel form of transport the coach houses still contained a victoria, a barouche, a single and a double brougham, a dog-cart, a waggonette which carried the three maids in the laundry by the shore to Kirkoswald church on Sundays, a bath chair that could be drawn by a donkey, and a cart for running errands.

There was novel sea transport in addition to the boats which supplied the castle with fish. The Marquess founded the Ailsa ship-yard at Troon, and personally designed and built racing yachts. A display of models and paintings of these commemorate the man who was responsible for the establishment of yacht building on the Clyde. The surrounding woodlands also bear witness to his enthusiasm for forestry. A high walled garden contains exotic trees and today a forestry exhibition has been mounted in its Victorian greenhouse.

The third Marquess presided over an Indian summer at Culzean, but the sun was setting by the time he died in 1938, to be succeeded by each of his three sons in turn. Two world wars during their lifetime eroded the basis of such lifestyles as this, as inexorably as the salt winds were eroding the stonework of Adam's castle. By the time the fifth Marquess succeeded in 1943, there was every prospect that the family would be compelled to retire to their older castle of Cassellis, leaving Culzean to revert to its original state of nature, a romantic ruin in its midst. Such was the threat when he offered the property to the National Trust for Scotland, without any endowment.

The war in Europe had just ended in May 1945, leaving an impoverished nation with more urgent buildings to repair than stately homes. The National Trust for Scotland had been invested with its authority by a private Act of Parliament ten years earlier, but it possessed a membership of only 1200 and correspondingly limited resources. When in November 1945 the Trust had the temerity to accept such a daunting responsibility as the custody of Culzean, nobody could be certain whether the property would make or break the fledgling organisation. However, the next forty years were to prove a tremendous success story.

A condition of the handover of Culzean was that the top floor of the castle should be converted into a National Guest Flat, and offered to General Dwight D. Eisenhower for life as a gesture of gratitude from the Scottish people. He arrived on his first visit in the autumn of 1946 with members of his family. Later he was to write: 'Twenty-one years ago I was offered and gladly accepted the gift for my lifetime of the National Guest Flat at Culzean Castle. At that time I assured the

Scottish Trust that nothing else that Scotland could have done could so emphatically symbolise for me the feeling of British-American partnership which was such a vital force in bringing the war to a successful conclusion. The better I have come to know the Scottish people the stronger has been my affection for them and for Culzean.'

During those intervening decades Culzean had been transformed. But in the early days the financial situation was so precarious that it was feared Culzean might drive the National Trust for Scotland into liquidation. Rescue came from government grants, the help of private trusts and much voluntary support. From the time when the castle was first opened to the public on 1 May 1947, the subscriptions of Trust members and fees paid by visitors swelled gradually. Today Culzean attracts far larger crowds than any other Trust property, of which there are now a hundred.

None of these others has required so much skill and money to restore. Much of its stone fabric was very severely weathered, and the local quarries from which the stone had been brought were exhausted. The work of replacing carved detail and giving a new surface skin to the damaged areas of the building was begun in 1966 and still continues, using stone brought from Durham.

The restoration of the interior had to wait until later. It was begun in 1972, and was based on a careful examination of Robert Adam's papers, as well as an exploration of what lay behind wallpapers and paint applied since his day. The most spectacular triumph of all this care and skill is the great saloon. Here the original colours of the ceiling, recovered when Adam's sketch was traced, have been replaced. The priceless circular carpet, made locally to his design, has been entrusted to the care of the Royal Scottish Museum in Edinburgh. But a facsimile, incorporating the same Kennedy swan motif, has been made to replace it.

The balustrades of the oval stairway and of the balconies above are sustained by 168 supports containing a Greek vase design. Every one of them was removed and stripped of the gilt paint that had been applied to them, to reveal the different metals in their composition. The work was carried out by a team provided by the Manpower Services Commission, and this body was also responsible for the repair and refurbishing of the weapons that hang in the entrance hall armoury.

But there was to be an altogether novel addition to the interior. Eisenhower returned to Culzean in 1959 as President of the United

States. No other nation in Europe had paid him such a compliment as Scotland had done in providing him with a home here, and he responded with generosity, in which his countrymen shared. This was expressed through the body that became known as Scottish Heritage USA, which has gradually established closer links with Culzean and the Trust. When President Eisenhower suggested that his flat should be made available to others, and thus become a source of income to the Trust, it was the directors of Scottish Heritage who set about implementing this proposal.

Eisenhower's most imaginative gesture of appreciation, however, was his offer in 1965 to donate some of his personal possessions to Culzean, as souvenirs of his visits. Out of this evolved the castle's Eisenhower exhibition room. It contains the desk at which he planned the North Africa landing, the ship's clock and barometer he used when he was commanding SHAPE, a replica of the vase that was presented to him by his White House staff when he retired from the Presidency, and many other personal mementoes. These are contained in a room that was constructed as nearly as possible to resemble the office he used as Supreme Commander. Before visitors reach it, they pass a display which tells the story of his life in words and pictures. Dwight D. Eisenhower died in March 1969; the Eisenhower memorial exhibition was dedicated on 8 May 1970, the twenty-fifth anniversary of VE Day.

While this new focus of interest was being created within the castle, one of an altogether different kind was evolving without. In 1967 the Countryside (Scotland) Act was placed on the statute book, and two years later Culzean was designated Scotland's first country park. It was a pioneer venture also in that responsibility for managing the park was to be shared with three local authorities, the Ayrshire County Council and the Burghs of Ayr and Kilmarnock, supported by the Scottish Development Department and the Countryside Commission, although ownership would remain in the hands of the Trust. This arrangement has given the lie to the saying that too many cooks spoil the broth. Scotland's first country park was recently called 'certainly the most magnificent in Britain', a judgment that it would be hard to refute.

The centre from which it operates is amongst the most remarkable achievements of collective effort here. In 1777 Robert Adam built a home farm to the north of the castle which demonstrated that he could do more than design exquisite drawing rooms and other amenities of gracious living. Here he provided stabling for horses, housing for pigs, byres for crops, sheds for farm carts, accommodation for farm workers. Four turreted archways in the corners of a quadrangle led into its enclosed courtyard. This was surrounded by open arches that gave access to the various buildings. Taller crow-stepped gabled blocks extended behind them, forming the arms of a cross.

This complex, the most remarkable of its kind and period in the country, had been designed for an entirely functional purpose, for all the beauty of its proportions. It had become exceedingly dilapidated, and the task of repairing it and adapting it to the needs of a park centre was both complicated and costly. While skilled masons went to work between 1971 and 1974 the Scottish Development Department shouldered three quarters of the expense. The result is that Culzean now possesses incomparable headquarters for the ultimate extension to the amenities of this property.

The centre with its theatre, lecture rooms, exhibitions of local geology, marine biology, ornithology, agricultural history and much besides, serves a country park in which students can go out to explore for themselves, whether down to the shore or in the tree-top walk or at the pond. There are qualified rangers to guide visitors, and sign-posts direct those who wish to explore for themselves. This little tract of earth in Robert Burns country, in which there stands one of the most complete examples of Robert Adam's inspiration, has clearly not lost its magic.

GLAMIS

Between the Braes of Angus and the Sidlaw hills the Vale of Strathmore runs north-east, Perth beyond its lower end, Montrose where the strath opens towards the sea. Angus was one of the seven Celtic earldoms and is thought to have been a Pictish kingdom in the Dark Ages. The darkness is lit by the rich collection of Pictish sculptures, especially those preserved in the Meigle museum a few miles from Glamis. There is a particularly fine cross-slab only a few hundred yards from Glamis Castle gates, ornamented with intricate interlace and containing the mysterious Pictish symbols, with a great salmon carved on its reverse side.

It was at Dunnichen in Angus that the Pictish King Brudei inflicted a crushing defeat on the Angles in 685, after both Edinburgh and Stirling had been captured by them. But there was no stone castle at Glamis then, nor for many centuries after. The castle first took the form of a fourteenth-century L-shaped tower, whose proportions can still be seen in the vaults that filled its two wings. The oldest stairway in the building descends, with treacherously uneven steps, to the mediaeval well and kitchens below them.

The smaller of the two vaults is known as Duncan's Hall, and legend tells that the King was murdered here by Macbeth in 1040. But King Duncan is known to have met his death in Moray, far to the north, apart from the fact that the vault had not yet been built. On the other hand, it is extremely likely that Duncan came hunting here, and it may well be that a royal hunting lodge stood on the site at the time. It is noteworthy that when the first stone castle was erected, it was not placed in a more defensible position on any of the surrounding slopes, but here in the valley bottom, convenient for gatherings of huntsmen.

By 1264 at the latest, Glamis had become a royal thanage, for that is when it appears first in public record. A thanage was a hereditary office, deriving from the older Celtic office of *Toiseach*, which survives in the name Mackintosh. Its incumbent was empowered to exercise the royal authority in the area. In 1372 the first Stewart sovereign Robert II bestowed the thanage of Glamis on Sir John Lyon, a few years before he married the King's daughter Joanna. The origins of the first Lyon of Glamis are uncertain, but it seems likely that he descended from the aristocracy of the Gaelic west. After the royal marriage his thanage was erected into a feudal barony and he was invested with the highest office of state as Chamberlain of Scotland. Like the Kennedys of Culzean and others who descended from a Stewart princess, the family bore the tressure flory counter-flory on their coat-of-arms, which also surrounds the lion rampant of the royal arms.

Robert II reared at least twenty-one children, and he bestowed another of his daughters on David Lindsay, whom he created Earl of Crawford. The brothers-in-law quarrelled, and Crawford murdered the Thane of Glamis. However, their descendants were more amicable, and the larger of the two crypts contains a somewhat eerie souvenir of their association. It is a secret chamber in the prodigious thickness of the wall, in which the first Lyon of Glamis to be created a peer of Parliament used to play cards with the fourth Earl of Crawford. They did so, furthermore, on the Sabbath in the company of the devil, but such scandalous behaviour did not prevent Patrick, Lord Glamis from being appointed a Privy Councillor, and even Master of the Household by James II in 1450. Nevertheless, there were uncanny happenings in the vault, which were only terminated when the chamber was sealed up. Its window can still be seen on the outside of the castle.

Many mediaeval keeps of this kind had their entrance on an upper floor, reached by a ladder that could be removed in an emergency. But at Glamis it may be that there was always a ground-floor entrance, where a stout iron yett still guards the door in the angle-tower. Within, a circular stone stair wound its way past the vaults to the great hall above. It was sealed off when wider stairs were built, but these still lead to the oldest remaining chambers in the castle, the vaults known as the crypt and Duncan's Hall. Their stonework is unadorned by plaster or paint, and today they are museums of armour and weaponry, pewter and furniture of impressive age, though none so old as the stout walls around them.

Glamis was taken back into the possession of the Crown in circumstances which all but extinguished the Lyon family. John the sixth Lord Glamis married Janet, sister of Archibald Douglas, the sixth Earl of Angus. It was an impressive alliance, but Lord Glamis died in 1528, leaving his young widow with a baby son. She made a second marriage with Alexander Campbell of Skipnish, and all might have been well, had not her brother the Earl of Angus married the widowed Queen Margaret after her husband James IV was killed on the field of Flodden.

Her son James V grew up with a hatred for his stepfather which extended to everyone of the name of Douglas. In 1537 he accused the former Lady Glamis, her second husband, her young son and her two brothers of being 'art and part of the treasonable conspiration and imagination of the slaughter and destruction of our sovereign lord's most noble person by poison'. Lady Glamis was also charged with employing witchcraft, and burnt alive as a witch in front of Edinburgh castle. She was a beautiful woman of impeccable character, and the fortitude with which she bore her ordeal touched many hearts.

Her second husband was killed when he fell from the castle rock, in an attempt to escape. But the seventh Lord Glamis was granted a stay of his death sentence until he should reach his majority. Meanwhile his property was forfeited, and from 1537 until 1542 King James V and his Queen, Mary of Lorraine, held court at Glamis. The King melted down the twelve silver flagons of Glamis, each weighing twelve pounds.

In Duncan's Hall hang separate portraits of the royal pair, supposed to have been painted here during one of their periods of residence. They possess none of the quality of the fine dual portraits in Blair Castle and Falkland Palace, and are such poor likenesses that their authenticity has been questioned. In the castle dining room there are also copies of the chairs of state which the sovereigns occupied during their visits.

Salvation came to the Lyons through the untimely death of James V in 1542, and the sense of justice of his excellent Queen Mary of Lorraine, to whom authority passed. The young heir was released and restored to his property in 1543 by formal Act of Parliament. So the seventh Lord Glamis possessed the necessary endowment to make a marriage as prestigious as that of his father, to a sister of the fourth Earl Marischal whose castle of Dunnottar stood on its rock up the coast to the north, near Stonehaven.

The seventh Lord Glamis died two years before Mary Queen of Scots returned from France in 1561, so it was his son who welcomed her to the castle in 1562 when she paid her visit in 'extreme foul and cold weather'. Her spirits were undamped, as one of her entourage remarked, 'I never saw her merrier, never dismayed.' He heard her declare that she longed to be a man, 'to lie all night in the fields, or to walk upon the causeway with a pack or knapschall (head-piece), a

Glasgow buckler, and a broadsword'. She was on her way north to clip the wings of the obstreperous Gordons of Huntly, which helps to explain her martial attitude.

John Lyon, eighth Lord Glamis, was appointed Chancellor of Scotland in 1573, when Mary's son James VI was a child of six. But a few years later he met his death as he was passing out of Stirling Castle and encountered the Earl of Crawford with his retinue on the causeway. There was a scuffle in which Lord Glamis was killed by one of Crawford's men, leaving his three-year-old son Patrick as his heir.

The boy possessed a redoubtable uncle in Sir Thomas Lyon, who managed his affairs so efficiently as the Tutor of Glamis that the English ambassador described the family as enjoying 'the greatest revenue of any baron in Scotland'. From 1585 Sir Thomas also controlled the national finances as Lord Treasurer. The King had learned both to respect and to fear him from an early age. Once, when the little monarch had attempted to leave his presence in Stirling Castle, Sir Thomas put out his leg and tripped him up. King James burst into tears, and received no more comfort than, 'better bairns greet than bearded men'.

The Tutor sent his ward Lord Glamis to improve his education on a European tour when he was only eight years old. The castle contains a portrait of this handsome youth, painted in France by François Clouet. His little secretary George Boswell is depicted on the reverse side of the panel, a quill behind his ear. A scroll beside his head reads:

> *My Lord I am at your command*
> *As was my father's will*
> *That I suld be ane trew servand*
> *And yet I will fulfill*
> *Quhat you command eik*
> *I shall do my devoir.*

James VI frequently visited Glamis Castle in his youth, and developed an affection for its owner, who was eight years younger than himself. It is one of the more attractive aspects of this King's infatuations that he liked to play an almost paternal part in the marriages of his favourites. So it was with the ninth Lord Glamis, whose wedding James organised in the palace of Linlithgow 'with great triumph'. On the King's accession to the throne of England in 1603, the twenty-eight-year-old Lord Glamis accompanied him to London.

Three years later he was created Earl of Kinghorne, a far from niggardly reward for the duties of Captain of the Guard and Privy Councillor. His uncle had been stripped of the office of Lord Treasurer in 1593, and received no such favours. When he died in 1608 the King declared 'that the boldest and hardiest man of his dominions was dead'.

The Earl added a large wing to the four-storey tower he had inherited, with a round angle turret. He also remodelled the fourteenth century keep and embellished its banqueting hall with plasterwork said to have been devised by Inigo Jones. But he died when he was only forty in 1615, ten years before his sovereign. His son the second Earl was nineteen years old when he succeeded. He married Margaret Erskine, daughter of the Earl of Mar, and placed their monograms on the vaulted ceiling of the hall, which he continued to decorate.

It was said of the second Earl that 'coming to his inheritance the wealthiest peer in Scotland, he left it the poorest'. This was because he spent almost his entire fortune in subsidising the army of the Covenant which opposed the high church policies of Charles I. It was fortunate that he died of the plague in 1646 (the year in which King Charles capitulated to his Scottish opponents) leaving a three-year-old child to succeed him. He would only have been sixty-four if he had lived until Charles II was restored to his throne, while his heir was too young to become involved in the hazards of the interregnum.

But the estate was bankrupt, and to make matters worse the widowed Countess married the Earl of Linlithgow, and between them they plundered the property of all they could carry out of it. Commonwealth troops quartered themselves in the ransacked castle. The teenage Earl made his home in Castle Lyon near Longforgan, now known as Huntly Castle, when he returned from St Andrews university. Even here, he was obliged to borrow a bed from the minister to sleep in.

He brought his wife to Glamis in 1670 where, although they found the castle dilapidated and almost destitute of furniture, they ensconced themselves in some upper rooms. The estate was burdened by such colossal debts that they were advised it was beyond redemption. The third Earl accepted the challenge, and the castle as we see it today stands as a monument to the forty years of determination and skill that saved it from ruin.

He is believed by some to have been his own architect as well as his own business manager, as he found the means to transform Glamis into one of the most exuberant of seventeenth-century Scottish baronial mansions. This he did by adding a north-west wing, corresponding to the one that the first Earl, his grandfather, had built on the opposite side of the central complex. He kept a detailed record in which he defined his objectives.

'Though it be an old house, and consequently was the more difficult to reduce the place to any uniformity, yet I did covet extremely to order my building so as the frontispiece might have a resemblance on both sides.' He raised the central tower to a height of a hundred feet, the view from its summit extending from the Sidlaw hills in the south to the Grampians in the north, with the entire vale of Strathmore between. A two-storey superstructure was placed upon the main block of the castle, bristling with projecting turrets and conical roofs. Below them, the former L-shaped fortress, now with its north-west wing, spread out in the form of a Z-shaped palace.

The Earl lavished his care on the great hall that his grandfather and father had adorned. He described it as 'a room that I have ever loved', and well he might. Its magnificent fireplace is surmounted by a representation of the royal arms between caryatids, symbol of the jurisdiction that his family exercised in the King's name. At one end a large painting of the Earl with his three sons dominates this splendid room. He is dressed in a costume even more bizarre than that of the Marquess of Atholl, masquerading as Julius Caesar in Blair Castle.

The chapel is perhaps his finest contribution to the restorations at Glamis. The new decorations of its interior were completed in time for the chapel to be dedicated in 1688, before the revolution brought William and Mary to the throne and established a Presbyterian national church in Scotland. Today the chapels of Glamis and Roslin are the only two in which the Episcopal liturgy survives from before that event. This is a curious achievement on the part of a man whose father had ruined himself in opposing that very liturgy when Charles I sought to impose it on his nation.

The paintings in the chapel are the work of Jacob de Wett, a Dutchman who was employed by Sir William Bruce when he was reconstructing Holyroodhouse. The thirty-four paintings of Christ and his apostles that he executed here blaze from the walls of this little panelled room and invest it with great beauty. The apostles include Scotland's patron Saint Andrew, carrying two fish and his saltire-shaped cross. Christ is shown in the garden of the sepulchre with Mary Magdalene. De Wett has given him the features of Charles I and invested them with an expression of gentleness and resignation. Most oddly, he has depicted the Saviour in a wide-brimmed hat. In his delineation of the last supper, de Wett has painted the Apostle John, to whom the original Celtic church paid such special devotion, with his head resting on the breast of Christ.

In this chapel the spectre of the sixth Lady Glamis, burnt as a witch, has been seen, dressed in grey.

The third Earl married Helen, the Earl of Middleton's daughter, who embroidered bed hangings in *petit point*, animals, birds and fruit stitched into linen, with floral bands along the edges. These now hang in what is known as King Malcolm's room, beneath a ceiling embellished with the cipher of the second Earl and his wife Margaret Erskine, like that of the great hall. His coat-of-arms is depicted above the fireplace, which contains a great curiosity: panels of it are made of embossed leather that has the appearance of wood. The arms are less of a curiosity. As in so many of these mansions, the family could scarcely turn in any direction without being faced by their heraldry, and even when they finished the food on their plates they were generally reassured by the sight of the family blazon on their porcelain.

The portrait of the third Earl in the great drawing room depicts him pointing to the castle as he remodelled it, with its fanciful fortified approach. This contained three successive gates, beyond the last of which lay a courtyard surrounded by walls. The entrance in the central tower was adorned with Corinthian pilasters. On either side stood statues of the four Stewart Kings from the reign of James VI, the work of Arnold Quellin, one of the most fashionable sculptors of his time.

The Earl also placed a twenty-one foot high sundial in the grounds, a wonder of Baroque invention and technological skill. Between twisted columns on its octagonal base stand four lions, pointing to the four quarters of the compass, each with a dial in its paws. One of the dials is elliptical, one round, one rectangular and the other square. Above the lions there is a globe with facets in three tiers, a face for every week in the year. The time can be told at all seasons with remarkable accuracy, though local time according to the sundial is twelve minutes behind that of Greenwich, because it stands on a spot three degrees west of the Greenwich meridian.

The third Earl of Kinghorne obtained a new charter which defined with greater precision his possessions as the Earl of Strathmore, as well being the Earl of the royal burgh of Kinghorne. He died in 1696, and in the following year the son to whom he had bequeathed these augmentations to his home and title added the stone bridge which spans the River Dean in the castle grounds.

All of these amenities were placed at risk when the young fifth Earl joined the Jacobite uprising in 1715. At the battle of Sherriffmuir he was deserted by his men, but he and fourteen gallant companions seized and defended the Colour until he was hit by a musket shot and sabred by a dragoon. His death left his sixteen-year-old brother as the sixth Earl and it was he who welcomed the Old Chevalier as James VIII when he arrived at Glamis in 1716, his cause already lost. The Pretender arrived in the company of his incompetent commander the Earl of Mar and an entourage of eighty-eight others, for whom accommodation had to be found.

In the chapel, the *de jure* King of Scots touched sufferers from scrofula, known as the King's Evil, and it was believed that he was able to cure them. The bed in which he slept is still preserved at Glamis, as well as a sword on which is inscribed: 'God save James VIII, prosperitie to Scotland and No Union'. His silver watch is also to be seen here, which he left under his pillow by mistake. A servant stole it, but her descendant gave it back to the Strathmore family.

The Pretender's young host the sixth Earl was not punished for his hospitality to the Jacobites, but he came to a violent end in the town of Forfar five miles away, in 1728. Lady Nairne described the rather mysterious episode. The culprit was James Carnegie of Finavon. 'It was Finavon who, without any previous warning, ran through and through the body (and no sword drawn but his own) as he was walking on the street in Forfar after a burial he had been at. Whether it was premeditated malice or mad fury, I know not.' So it was his younger brother who had the dubious privilege of welcoming Butcher Cumberland on his way north to fight the Battle of Culloden. He is said to have slept in the same bed as the Pretender thirty years earlier.

Subsequent embellishments to the interior of the castle celebrate the ninth Earl's marriage with the heiress Mary Bowes. Her name was associated originally with Bowes castle in Yorkshire, now a ruin. It was carried across the Border when Sir Robert Bowes raided Teviotdale in 1542, at the outset of Henry VIII's Rough Wooing of the baby Mary Queen of Scots. He was captured, but released. Another Sir

Robert Bowes came to Edinburgh as the English ambassador later in the same century.

The family seat was Streatlam castle when Sir William Bowes married the daughter and heiress of Sir William Blakiston, the last baronet of Gibside. So it came about that after Sir William's granddaughter Mary married the ninth Earl, the great fireplace of Gibside was carried to Glamis, where it adorns the billiard room. The ramifications of all these prosperous alliances can be read, as usual, in the bright colours of heraldry. The Gibside fireplace displays the Blakiston arms, both impaled and quartered, while below it are firescreens that present the newly quartered arms of the Earls of Strathmore, the blue lion rampant and the three bows.

The billiard room, which belongs to the seventeenth century additions to the castle, contains tapestries of that era. Those depicting Nebuchadnezzar are of especial interest, while others that show Abraham preparing to sacrifice Isaac, and Jacob cheating Esau are curious in their own way. Perhaps they are the work of daughters of the house. The glory of the billiard room is the great painting at the end opposite the fireplace, *The Fruit Market* by Rubens and Snyders.

It was the ninth Earl who made the alterations to the grounds which so incensed Sir Walter Scott that he wrote: 'It is thirty years and upwards since I have seen Glamis, but I have never yet forgotten or forgiven the atrocity which under pretence of improvement deprived that lordly place of its appropriate accompaniments, leaving an ancient dome and towers like these beggared and defaced.'

The outer court was removed, with the second and third gates. So were the four Stewart kings, which were discovered later 'along with other figures, lying out of sight, sadly mutilated. They are fine works of art and are worthy of a better fate.' The effigies of James VI and Charles I have since been repaired and restored to their former positions, while the other two have disappeared without trace. They face the castle in an open lawn at the end of a long avenue of trees, for the defensive walls were also removed. But the third Earl's gateways were re-erected at the north and south entrances to the castle grounds.

The ninth Earl died in 1776, and it was during the lifetime of his heir that the disaster occurred to which these old houses were prone in the days of open fires and candlelight. The entire wing which the first Earl had added to the original tower early in the seventeenth century was gutted by fire in 1800, and it was not until the twelfth

Earl had succeeded in 1846 that it was restored. The room on its first floor was refurbished as the dining room, the overmantel of its oak fireplace decorated with the twelfth Earl's coat-of-arms untinctured. All around the walls the diners could inspect the impaled arms of past members of the family in their heraldic colours, testifying to its past alliances. Even the stained glass windows recorded the evolution of the Strathmore achievement.

The portraits on the walls commemorate those who dined here. Among these is the thirteenth Earl, who was six years old when George IV died, and lived on into the reign of Edward VII. It was he who inaugurated a return to an earlier style of horticulture at Glamis when he laid out the Dutch garden beside the third Earl's north-west wing. Roses bloom within miniature box hedges between gravel walks. In their centre, Mercury the messenger of the gods is arrested in full flight, with wings on his sandals and serpent-circled wand.

This creative interest in the gardens was inherited by his son, the subject of one of the most attractive dining-room portraits. The fourteenth Earl is depicted with his wife Cecilia Cavendish Bentinck, the Duke of Portland's daughter, in the great drawing room. Over-looking them from the far end of the hall is the third Earl, the painting of him with his three sons reproduced in miniature, a picture within a picture. It was this pair who created the Italian garden beyond the Dutch one, two acres laid out in a seventeenth-century style within yew hedges, containing gravelled walks, herbaceous borders, gazebos and a fountain.

Countess Cecilia embroidered a bed canopy in which she stitched the names of all her ten children. Among these was Lady Elizabeth Bowes-Lyon, born in 1900. In 1923 she was married to King George V's second son the Duke of York, and thirteen years later she became the first Scottish Queen Consort for many hundreds of years. During the intervening centuries the wives of British kings had been selected from among foreign princesses, not all of whom had been reared in palaces as magnificent as Glamis or could boast the same royal descent as that of Queen Elizabeth from the dynasties of Bruce, Stewart and Hanover. Her accession with her husband King George VI marked a new departure. The manner in which she has fulfilled the role thrust upon her so suddenly by the abdication of King Edward VIII has earned her a unique place in the hearts of her subjects. There can be no doubt that many of the visitors to Glamis come especially to see the home in which she was reared.

Here have been preserved the suite of rooms set aside by the Earl and Countess for their daughter and her husband when they were Duke and Duchess of York. The Duke's bedroom contains the bed made for the first Earl early in the seventeenth century, its canopy decorated with his coat-of-arms. The seventeenth-century four-poster in the bedroom furnished for the Duchess contains the monogram of her parents on its head-board, and on the inside of its canopy she could see above her head the names of all her brothers and sisters, stitched by her mother. Portraits of them hang on the walls, as well as the famous painting of herself by de Laszlo.

The Queen Mother's sitting room, with its tapestries, its porcelain, and the blending colours of its curtains, chair covers and cushions, gives an intimate glimpse of her personal taste. Here we are in an ancient part of the castle, as the thickness of the entrances and window embrasures suggests. At the entrance to the Queen Mother's sitting room there is a small stone seat on which the figure of a boy servant has been seen, awaiting orders. How long he has been in attendance no one knows.

Naturally there are mementoes of the Queen Mother's children here also. On either side of the fireplace in the great drawing room are the seats on which they used to sit as little girls. As for their mother's childhood, there is a picture of her at a children's party, with one of her brothers. He is dressed in a miniature copy of the jester's costume that was made for the third Earl's fool in the seventeenth century, perhaps the only suit of motley that survives from that age.

To celebrate the eightieth birthday of Queen Elizabeth the Queen Mother in 1980, wrought iron gates were made for the entrance to the Italian garden that her parents had created. They were fashioned by the local blacksmith George Sturrock and decorated with roses and thistles, as well as the year in which the Queen Mother came to open them for the first time.

Her relatives the seventeenth Earl and Countess of Strathmore and Kinghorne still live in a wing of the castle. But today anyone may come to examine the treasures of the home in which she was brought up, and enjoy its gardens and grounds. Not many of them, probably, will share the feelings of Sir Walter Scott as the magnificent spectacle of Glamis Castle comes into view in the distance.

BRODIE

'This castle hath a pleasant seat.' The nearest such building to the heath on which Macbeth is reputed to have encountered the witches is Brodie. From its tower the Grampian mountains can be seen to the south, while Findhorn Bay opens into the Moray Firth to the north. The fertile lands of Moray surround Brodie Castle on every hand, basking in one of the mildest climates of the British Isles, rare in such a latitude.

Beside one of the drives to the castle stands a ninth-century Pictish stone, a cross decorated by intricate interlace on one of its faces. On the other are some of the fourteen Pictish symbols that have defied every attempt to interpret their meaning with certainty. On the rim of the stone is an equally inscrutable inscription in the Ogham script. This monument was discovered buried in the ground at Dyke, which belonged to the Brodie domain at least from the date of the charter bestowed by Alexander III, who died in 1286.

By this time, other notable families had moved up from the south, and planted themselves in north-east Scotland: Grants and Frasers, Cummings and the Roses of the neighbouring castle of Kilravock. The Gordons were to arrive later. In all these cases, their origins and the date of their arrival are known with certainty. The Brodies are different. There is neither historical evidence nor tradition to account for their presence here as colonists from somewhere else. For all we know, they could have been present when King Brudei received Saint Columba in nearby Inverness during the sixth century. The Pictish symbols may have defined their property and status long before the first royal charter did so. If Macbeth really did meet witches in the grounds of Brodie when he was King of Moray, it is not unlikely that Brodies were in his company.

What is certain is that they have been living here for at least eight hundred years, and that no less than twenty-five Thanes of Brodie have followed one another during that period of time in male descent. The title of Thane replaced the older Celtic term Toiseach early in the Middle Ages, and the Brodies seem to have been content to enjoy it to the exclusion of any more new-fangled hereditary rank. At any rate, they did not exploit the opportunities that were open to them from time to time, to bid for a peerage.

A little over four hundred years ago they built themselves a new home of the Z plan design that was fashionable during the sixteenth century. The original structure evolved over a period of generations, and it has been altered and enlarged during the centuries. This castle seems to assert that no Brodie of Brodie ever took a notion to remove anywhere else, nor would submit willingly to a forcible removal. Originally it contained neither door nor windows on the ground floor; only gun-loops, such as can still be seen in the vaulted guard chamber beside a ground-floor entrance that was introduced later.

The need for such precautions was brought home to Alexander, the fifteenth Thane of Brodie, after he had succeeded to the property in 1632. It was he who embellished the vaulted ceiling of what is now the blue sitting room with decorative plasterwork. The central pendant here takes the form of the Brodie crest, a hand grasping arrows, though this was added later. Alexander Brodie's initials, and those of his wife Elizabeth Innes, are included in the design and their arms are displayed above the fireplace. Elizabeth died when her husband was only twenty-three years old, but she had provided a son and he never remarried during the remaining forty years of his life.

In the year of his bereavement, 1640, he gave expression to his religious principles by taking a party of men to the most magnificent cathedral built in this latitude of Scotland, the Lantern of the North at Elgin. There they piously mutilated the carvings in wood and stone, and destroyed paintings of the Crucifixion and the Last Judgment. Brodie supported the army of the Covenant in the rebellion against Charles I, thus exposing his home to a similar fate.

Nemesis struck in 1645 when Lord Lewis Gordon, the gallant companion of Montrose, swept down on the stronghold of the devout Covenanter, captured it, and set the place on fire. The ceiling of the blue room escaped the blaze, but it seems likely that the plasterwork of the great hall was injured beyond repair. Most seriously, almost the entire muniments were destroyed, depriving this family and neighbourhood of their historical records. A solitary missive from King Robert Bruce escaped, referring to the property of Dyke in which the Pictish symbol stone was subsequently discovered.

After the execution of Charles I, Brodie was one of the Commissioners despatched by the Scottish Presbyterians to invite his son Charles II to be crowned at Scone as a Covenanted King. Charles was soon defeated and fled back into exile, where he nursed an abiding hatred for those who had bored him with their dogmatic homilies and insulted his father and mother to his face. Presbyterianism, he declared, was not the religion of a gentleman.

Brodie, for his part, 'resolved and determined in the strength of the Lord to eschew and avoid all employment under Cromwell'. This was not due to patriotism, but because Cromwell refused to impose Presbyterianism on those who held other beliefs. After the King's restoration in 1660, Brodie went to London in the expectation of royal favour, only to be dismissed with a swingeing fine. Back at his castle he continued to keep a copious diary which not only preserves a valuable account of some of the events of his time, but also an introspective account of the state of his soul.

He had escaped the fate of his leading co-religionist, the Marquess of Argyll, who was executed. His house and estate, battered and impoverished, passed to his son who married Lady Mary Kerr. Her father the Earl of Lothian had been a fellow Commissioner with Alexander Brodie when they visited Charles at Breda and invited him to his kingdom. The pair witnessed the triumph of their fathers' faith in the revolution of 1688. Presented with nine daughters by his noble wife, the sixteenth Thane married the eldest of them to her cousin George Brodie, who consequently succeeded in 1708 as the seventeenth of the line.

Mystery surrounds the restoration of the castle he inherited. Its most flamboyant new embellishment was the heavy plaster ceiling in what is now the dining room. This bears a superficial resemblance to the magnificent baroque ceiling with which the Duke of Lauderdale adorned his castle of Thirlestane in the reign of Charles II. A closer parallel has been found in one of the royal palaces of Denmark. In the corners of the ceiling are curious emblems that have been interpreted as representations of the four elements of fire, earth, air and water. They are framed by deep ribs adorned with curling vines and grapes. A pelican in its piety fills one of the smaller spaces; so do the crown and thistle of Scotland, a unicorn and an angel with sun and crown. One of the mysteries is the large empty centre in this elaborate design. The whole is supported by a cornice and frieze that run round the tops of the walls.

Is it possible that the pious diarist could have commissioned such an essentially secular embellishment to his home, or that he would have wished to embark on such an extravagance even if he could have afforded it after having incurred a crippling fine? If he did not, then it was presumably his son who was responsible, despite the fact that he kept a diary also, which reveals an equally unworldly mind. His son-in-law, succeeding immediately after the incorporating Union of the kingdoms in 1707, seems only to have carried out some repairs before he was plunged into the dangers and expense of the Jacobite uprising in 1715.

Naturally the Brodies supported the Protestant succession of the House of Hanover, but they were surrounded by neighbours who did not. In September 1715 the Marquess of Huntly, heir to the Duke of Gordon, sent a demand for Brodie's arms and horses with the threat: 'If you are not content of these proposals I must let Lord Seaforth know. He and I are to take measures conjunct, according to your answer.' The Earl of Seaforth, Chief of the Mackenzies, posed as serious a threat from the north as the Chief of the Gordons from the south.

But further north still, there was the Gordon Earl of Sutherland, active in the Hanoverian interest. Brodie provided maintenance for 1200 men under his command when they were quartered on his property during their passage to Elgin, and again on their return. In addition, the castle was garrisoned by troops for two months. While all this was going on the seventeenth Thane died and was succeeded by his son James. The rising failed, the castle remained unscathed, and its muniments survived intact.

They have a sorry tale to tell. The Earl of Sutherland was rewarded with the office of Lord Lieutenant of Orkney and a generous pension of £1200 a year, while he defaulted on those who had trusted to his good faith. In December the Earl had written to Brodie from Inverness: 'It being absolutely necessary that this place should be well provided, and that the rebels should have as little to subsist upon as we can, I desire you may send hither all the meal and dried corn you possibly can.' Such requests had been honoured without demur.

By 1720 one of the Earl's other victims was writing to Brodie: 'It's a great affront on the Earl that we have been so long out of our money for serving him and government so faithfully.' The writer was particularly outraged because they had not demanded instant payment 'from the Earl per his particular order and receipts from the general adjutants and quartermasters'.

The eighteenth Thane died in the same year without receiving satisfaction and was succeeded by his brother Alexander. Early in

November 1721 he was one of no less than twenty-three signatories who commissioned a lawyer in Elgin to 'sue and uplift the sum or sums of money advanced and delivered in loan by us to John, Earl of Sutherland as Lord Lieutenant of this shire in the year 1715 for maintaining and carrying on the public service, conform to the receipts and other vouchers under the hand of the said Earl of Sutherland and others in his name.' In Brodie eyes, one Gordon may have appeared much like another, whatever his political complexion.

The portrait of Alexander Brodie of Brodie hangs below the baroque ceiling that has been dated to the seventeenth century. On the other hand, the dining room's marble mantelpiece belongs to about the year 1730. This was when an Elgin mason named John Ross began work at the castle, constructing its new staircase, more suited to the taste of this age (as well as to the ample dresses of the ladies) than the narrow circular stairways of stone.

For many decades the chamber with its elaborate plaster ceiling was used as a library. Today its table is set with an armorial dinner service that still contains a hundred and two surviving items. Recently a portion of the plasterwork fell on one of the porcelain plates, breaking it in pieces, which was less unfortunate than if it had struck a member of the visiting public. The castle houses no poltergeist, and the accident is unlikely to occur again.

Alexander the nineteenth Thane served as a Member of Parliament as some of his predecessors had done. He was a supporter of Archibald Campbell, the brilliant and eccentric man who became third Duke of Argyll and built the castle of Inveraray. Known as King of Scotland, Archibald might have assisted Brodie to a hereditary peerage as he did others of his friends. But the Thane was evidently content with the office of Lord Lyon King of Arms.

Not that he showed much interest in genealogy or heraldry. His enthusiasm, and that of his wife Mary Sleigh, was the improvement of his estate. The castle contains a possible portrait of this remarkable woman, but it is not a certain attribution. Their enterprises, like those of the Duke of Argyll, were placed at risk when the uprising of 1745 occurred. Once again, the Brodie papers survive to tell what occurred here.

Of the able Campbell commanders who opposed the Jacobites, it was the Earl of Loudoun who came to Inverness, where he was joined by Mackays from the far north as in the Fifteen. There he was supplied with meal from Brodie, while the soldiers of Prince Charles helped themselves to the crops of the estate as well when they had the opportunity. An account of the value of the provisions that went to both camps is preserved in the family archives. There seems to have been a respite until the Jacobites returned from their long march into England, and reached Inverness early in 1746.

By then Brodie Castle was garrisoned once more. In the absence of the Lord Lyon, his wife dispensed the supplies between February and April when the Battle of Culloden was fought. 'Straw for litter was given out in gross,' runs the account that was penned when the emergency was over. 'This article is not reckoned on, neither is the maintainance of the servants who were all quartered in the house; and as for the gentlemen their masters, they were all extremely welcome to the best this house could afford.'

No wonder. The Lord Lyon's first cousin James Brodie of nearby Spynie was meanwhile compelled to support the Jacobites. 'I have lost by them above one and a half free years' rent including my personal charges; besides multitudes living at my house who not only consumed all my year's provisions of every kind which I had laid in, but my wife was at great expense in buying all sorts of fresh meal for them, and if the Duke's speedy march from Spey had not surprised them, they were resolved to have burned all this country.' So he wrote on 21 May. Butcher Cumberland was execrated even by Hanoverians in the aftermath of Culloden, but there were those who were relieved to see him all the same.

The emergency over, the Brodies were able to resume their improvements to the castle and estate. Mary Sleigh's part was re-called with admiration after her death. 'This excellent Lady . . . had acquired liberal and comprehensive views of the benefit and mutual relations of agriculture, manufacture and commerce . . . The men she employed in levelling, trenching, draining and raising fences; and trained women to industry, by establishing a school for spinning and for dispensing premiums. She raised quantities of flax, encouraged her tenants to cultivate it, and built them a mill for bruising and scutching it.' The Thane and his wife beautified the castle policies, through which a long straight avenue to their home was laid and lined with lime trees. There was a formal pond, and twisting walks to Macbeth's hill.

In 1749 they were troubled once more by a Gordon. The Lord Lyon received a warning in the November of that year that 'a neigh-bour of yours is rearing up a double pigeon house on the skirt of a barren muir, remote from any considerable cornfield of his own, but immediately adjacent to a very fertile one of yours, both in barley and black grain: the gentleman has already no fewer than three very rich pigeon houses in the neighbourhood, a larger number than any other gentleman in the country has upon so narrow a tract of ground.' Under Scots law a proprietor was permitted to build a pigeon house (or dovecot) if his land yielded ten chalders of grain, a considerable amount. A dovecot was thus visible evidence of a man's wealth, very much a status symbol. In their rich variety of design, many have been preserved from this age, ornaments of the Scottish landscape. The Boath dovecot not far from Brodie is an attractive example.

Lyon petitioned the Lords of Session in Edinburgh in April 1750 'to suspend and discharge the procedure in the said intended dovecot'. The culprit, Sir Robert Gordon of Gordonstoun, objected in July 'that he has five or six chalders within two miles of the dovecot building by him'. The case dragged on to the end of 1751, doubtless fattening the lawyers in Edinburgh better than Brodie's corn could have fattened Gordon's pigeons. Ancient animosities were revived in a novel form.

In 1754 the Lord Lyon died, leaving his estate, heavily in debt, to a consumptive son of eighteen who died without issue five years later. The Thanage passed to a fifteen-year-old youth, grandson of the James Brodie of Spynie who had been fleeced by the Jacobites in the Forty-Five. After the young Thane came of age he eloped with Lady Margaret Duff, daughter of the Earl of Fife. Naturally she did not bring him the marriage portion he so urgently required in his straitened circumstances. By 1774 the twenty-first Thane was compelled to put his property on the market to pay his debts.

A Brodie of Brodie was no unfit husband for a Duff, but a Thane without a Thanage was a different matter. The Earl of Fife stepped in to purchase the property. He handed the barony of Brodie to his son-in-law but compensated himself by retaining some of the outlying lands. Twelve years later, after Margaret had borne her husband five children, tragedy struck the happy pair. She was sitting beside the fire in her night clothes, in what had been described as the best bedroom in the time of the Lord Lyon. It is the chamber in the end tower, above the dining room with its baroque ceiling. While Lady Margaret Brodie drowsed, a peat fell out of the grate, set fire to her dress and she was burned to death.

By the time this occurred in 1786, Brodie's brother Alexander had prospered in India, whither so many Scots went to seek their fortunes in this age. Brodie's son, heir to a diminished estate, joined his uncle in Madras, where a fine mansion called Brodie Castle still stands witness to their prosperity. He lived to beget seven children before he was drowned off Madras in a sailing accident. The twenty-first Thane lived for another twenty-two years after this second tragedy, the death of his heir.

But he was able to welcome his grandchildren when their mother brought them home from India, and he had a charming portrait of them all painted by John Opie before they returned there with her. In India she remarried, to Lieutenant General Sir Thomas Bowser, the Governor of Madras. By the time the little boy in Opie's painting succeeded as the twenty-second Thane, his cousin Elizabeth, the daughter of Alexander Brodie of Madras, had married the Marquess of Huntly, who became the fifth and last Duke of Gordon. It was a happy ending to the long tale of strife between Gordons and Brodies.

In the entrance hall of Brodie Castle there is a marble statue of Venus that once stood in Gordon Castle. Its inscription states that it was presented to the Marquess of Huntly in 1817 with gratitude from the Consul at Leghorn. Huntly had been promoted General in 1808, and succeeded his father as Duke of Gordon in 1827.

The Brodie heir went on a continental tour with the Huntlys in 1822 to 1823, and kept a journal of his experiences. It appears that his affluent background, provided by his step-father the Governor of Madras, his uncle Alexander of Brodie Castle in India, and his cousin at Gordon Castle in Scotland, prepared him ill to cope with the financial situation at Brodie. He had no sooner entered into his inheritance in 1824 before he conceived grandiose plans to enlarge his castle. By 1828 his factor was warning him that unless he made 'a prudent marriage' (in other words, found an heiress), he might face ruin. It took him almost ten years to do this, but then the day was saved. His wife was Elizabeth Baillie of Redcastle on the Black Isle, west of Brodie. She seems to have been somewhat plain and cantankerous, but her fortune paid for the new extensions to Brodie castle.

Ground floor windows were installed for the first time as part of the original structure. They lighted a new library, replacing the one that had been housed previously in what became the dining room. Many valuable books on botanical and scientific subjects had been sold during the hard times of the 1820s, but five thousand remained.

A singular curiosity of the library is a chair that belonged formerly to Deacon William Brodie. The Brodie chiefs possessed clansmen based conveniently in Edinburgh, in various capacities. There was, for instance, Ludovick Brodie, Writer to the Signet, who assisted the Thane to frustrate Sir Robert Gordon during the dovecot squabble. William Brodie inherited his father's cabinet-making business in the capital, and became a Deacon Councillor there.

But he was addicted to gambling, and was driven to plan daring burglaries in order to meet the expenses of this hobby. Finally one of his accomplices turned king's evidence, and Deacon Brodie was convicted of robbing the excise office in the Canongate and hanged in 1788. It was a ten days' wonder in Edinburgh when this pillar of society was exposed as a criminal. It is likewise curious that the Brodies of Brodie should have preserved this souvenir of their disreputable namesake.

Above the library was the new drawing room, entered from the chamber that had served the same purpose centuries earlier, the original great hall. Perhaps its character was entirely lost before it was redecorated in the 1840s. But at least it preserves the proportions of the principal room in the largest structure in the sixteenth-century Z plan, the central rod in the letter. The end where the Thane dined before a fire at his high table with his family was now given a gothic wooden fireplace extending from floor to ceiling around the grate. In its niches were placed carved Flemish figures two hundred years older. Beside this edifice, a door still leads to what had once been the Thane's private apartment, its vaulted ceiling adorned with the seventeenth-century plasterwork.

Called the red drawing room, the old hall is now in effect a picture gallery, from whose opposite end a door has been made through the thick wall to the new drawing room. It is spacious, lit by large windows. Its roof of wooden ribs was painted in a design of soft pastel shades in the 1860s, and has now been restored. Here hangs the Opie portrait of the children from Madras, and a copy of the Romney painting of Jane, Duchess of Gordon with her son, the fifth Duke, who married Elizabeth Brodie. Works by the seventeenth-century Dutch masters overflow into here from the gallery beyond. But one of the most beautiful of them, 'The Philosopher and his Pupils' painted in 1626 by Willem van der Vliet, hangs on a staircase landing.

The twenty-second Thane, who gave the castle its present appearance, was painted by James Currie in the dining room with his wife and three of his children, and the Opie portrait on the wall behind them. He lived to celebrate the marriage of his heir to Lady Eleanor Moreton, the Earl of Ducie's daughter, and to welcome the arrival into the world of his grandson Ian, the twenty-fourth Thane. Ian and his wife Violet Hope were able to make the last distinctive contribution to Brodie, inside and out.

Ian Brodie of Brodie was a professional soldier who served in the Scots Guards and the Lovat Scouts and died in 1943. Neither he nor his wife possessed a formal education in the fine arts. Yet such was their natural taste in this field that they were able to assemble a collection of pictures of their own choice, without great expense, which is now the delight and admiration of all who visit their former home. Totally unrelated to the paintings they inherited, these consist principally of eighteenth-century English watercolours, and of twentieth-century pictures by Scots, French and English artists. Here you may see MacTaggart in the company of Dufy and Nash. But although it has been given its own picture gallery, the collection is too large to be exhibited in its entirety at any one time.

Since Ninian Brodie succeeded his parents as the twenty-fifth Thane, some strange objects have come to light in his ancient home. He discovered the skeleton of a child in the recess of a windowless closet in which the family papers are kept. It was sent to Edinburgh for examination and diagnosed as an eighteenth-century exhibit that had been preserved for its scientific interest. No sinister or uncanny happenings are recorded in this happy house. It possesses no ghost: not even the unfortunate Lady Margaret has returned to haunt the best bedroom in which she was burned to death.

The most spectacular discovery was made in June 1970 by Mrs Helena Brodie of Brodie. She was exploring a loft in the old castle stables when she came upon a pile of books and pamphlets half hidden beneath pigeon droppings. They included precious volumes of sixteenth-century maps, and eighteenth-century pamphlets. But the jewel of the collections was a vellum Pontifical, perhaps over a thousand years old. If such were its age, it could have been written before St Margaret came to Scotland and married King Malcolm Canmore. Analysis reveals a connection with Canterbury, or perhaps with Durham, home of St Margaret's confessor and biographer Turgot. It predates by centuries the foundation of Elgin cathedral in 1224.

The Brodie Pontifical was acquired by the British Museum. Here it joined the company of the Saint John Gospel, buried with Saint

Cuthbert at Lindisfarne when he died in 687, and of the Lindisfarne Gospel Book. Unlike this, the Brodie Pontifical is not illuminated, its contents being directions for the conduct of divine service, accompanied by prayers and liturgies.

By the time it was discovered, the present Thane had already approached the National Trust for Scotland to discover whether his home could be transferred to its care. It was no longer feasible to maintain a castle and grounds of such size in private hands. By 1969 his heir was married and his first grandson had been born. The hereditary succession was secure in the male line for two more generations. But the future of the property was by no means so secure.

Ninian Brodie might have raised the much needed cash for its maintenance by selling his parents' art collection, just as his great-grandfather had disposed of valuable books. But this he refused to do. Finally, his own generosity was matched by that of public bodies, and the Trust took over the custody of the castle and 170 acres of its grounds in 1980. Then, as Brodie has described, 'for about twelve months all was dust, hammering and sawing, and the castle was encased in scaffolding', as the structure was reharled, the roof repaired, and restoration work such as the repainting of the drawing room ceiling carried out. Brodie moved to a wing in the newest part of the castle, where he could watch the process of transformation.

Now it is the turn of the grounds. In 1953 a gale seriously damaged the long avenue lined with lime and chestnut. The old trees have been cut down and new ones planted. Ninian Brodie's parents had raised no less than 426 species of daffodil here, and although these remain one of the seasonal delights of Brodie, many of the varieties have been lost. The kitchen garden is now being used in an attempt to rear them once more. Meanwhile both castle and grounds have become magnets for all kinds of activities, from archery to musical concerts, and many people who come here to walk in the footsteps of the past find that they have the twenty-fifth Thane of Brodie as their guide.

CRAIGIEVAR

The rivers of Don and Dee flow eastwards out of the Grampian mountains, embracing the city of Aberdeen as they enter the North Sea. In their course they water the fertile lands of the ancient earldom of Mar. The castles of Mar were erected to protect these rolling valleys from the mountain folk of the west as well as from predatory neighbours. Gradually the style defined as Scots baronial architecture evolved, and Aberdeenshire is especially rich in examples of it. There are Midmar Castle, built late in the sixteenth century, and Castle Fraser and Fyvie of only slightly later date. Kincardineshire contains Crathes Castle on Deeside, while Angus can boast of Glamis and that far smaller gem, Claypotts Castle. Others of especial interest include Kellie Castle in Fife and Amisfield Tower in Dumfriesshire. Scots baronial was the most distinctive and inventive vernacular architecture to be seen in the country since the age of the brochs, over a thousand years earlier.

The most perfectly preserved of these buildings was placed about three hundred feet below the thousand-foot summit of the hill of Craigievar, overlooking the water of Leochel as it flows northwards to the River Don above Alford. The earliest historical reference to this property occurs in a charter of 1457, still on display in the castle. It names the Mortimers as the owners, a family evidently long established here, although so little is known about them. They began the building of their L-shaped tower at Craigievar towards the end of the sixteenth century, when so many others were doing the same. But they ran into financial difficulties before the work was far advanced and sold their estate to William Forbes of the neighbouring property of Corse in 1610. His elder brother, Patrick Forbes of Corse Castle, was a devout supporter of the Protestant Reformation. Even after he had succeeded to his patrimony he continued to study theology, accepted ordination, and became the minister of Keith. When King James VI restored bishops he nominated Patrick to the see of Aberdeen, which he accepted with pious reluctance. His son and heir John Forbes became Professor of Divinity at Aberdeen university while his father ruled the diocese with scrupulous zeal.

It was left to the younger brother William to make his mark in the secular field. Several times Patrick lent him money to launch him on a career in commerce, but nothing came of it. Finally Patrick told William that he would advance no more without adequate security. According to family tradition, William came to his brother for a further loan, only to be asked who was his guarantor.

'God Almighty,' answered William. 'I have none other to offer.'

'Well, brother,' said Patrick, 'He is not to be rejected; you shall have the money; it is the first time that such a surety has been offered to me, but may God Almighty, your bondsman, prosper you and see that it does you good.'

It did. William made the fortune in trading with the Baltic ports that earned him the name of Danzig Willie, and enabled him to purchase the estate of Craigievar in 1610. He acquired a number of other properties as well, the most important of which, to the future fortunes of Craigievar, was the former Church domain of Fintray lower down the River Don.

The portrait of William reveals a man with a long, strong face; a large nose, large chin, large lips, large ears beneath close-cropped hair of a light brown colour. It is one of the pictures by the father of Scottish portraiture, George Jamesone, that hang at Craigievar. Likenesses of his brother Bishop Patrick and of Professor John his nephew are also preserved here.

It took Danzig Willie until 1626 to complete the home that has earned such praise from posterity. Stewart Cruden, Inspector of Ancient Monuments for Scotland, has remarked: 'as a testimony of taste Craigievar ranks with any representative building in Britain'. The late Dr Douglas Simpson wrote: 'As a work of art it claims a Scottish place in the front rank of European architecture.' In these circumstances it is all the more extraordinary that its designer should have failed to leave his signature on its stonework.

Yet he could not hide his light under a bushel entirely. In 1618, when he was remodelling Castle Fraser lower down the River Don, he inscribed his name I. BEL on a tablet. Thus he identified himself as a member of the family of master masons which included George Bell and his sons David and John. And the fantastic invention of the upper works of Castle Fraser reveals the same calligraphy in stone as that of Craigievar.

It is uncertain how much earlier work had been completed by the Mortimers before John Bell arrived here. Within the castle's sole

Previous page Brodie Castle; *above* The Red Drawing Room

Above The Blue Sitting Room; *below* The Dining Room ceiling

Craigievar Castle

Top The Queen's Room
Left The Hall
Right William Forbes of Menie
and Craigievar by George Jamesone

Above Fyvie Castle; *below* The Hall

The Gallery; *overleaf* Isabella Macleod, Mrs James Gregory by Sir Henry
Raeburn

entrance are vaulted rooms within the conventional L-plan base, and it is thought that here at least part of the structure may date from before Danzig Willie's purchase. One of these rooms contained the kitchen, whose original fireplace arch remains, although a modern stove has been placed beneath it. Other vaults were used to store provisions and here also was a dungeon.

The entrance is contained in a tower embedded in the angle of the L, square rather than round in shape. Its door is a modern copy of the original one, which was massive and iron studded and which could not be opened unless the yett within it was first drawn back. This mediaeval Scottish device, an iron grating of interlocking bars, provided a secure defence. Even if the door was smashed in, this obstacle remained and those within could fire through its bars. Other defensive features were rounded corners at every angle of the tower. These deprived an enemy of sharp corner stones to prize from their sockets while, aesthetically, they gave an attractive softness to the outlines of the building.

The walls lean almost imperceptibly inwards until suddenly, high in the air, they sprout in a riot of corner turrets and towers, erupting at different levels, their conical caps competing with the crow-stepped gables. It is the finest expression of the master mason's creative imagination in north-east Scotland. The exuberance of this display is matched by the ingenuity that has been lavished on the restricted space within the castle.

Its main staircase leads to the hall in the longer wing of the L-shaped building. This was described by Douglas Simpson as 'one of the most remarkable rooms in Scotland', and by those nineteenth-century experts MacGibbon and Ross as 'almost the only one in Scotland which retains its original features undisturbed'.

It is of mediaeval design, its high groined vault occupying two storeys, its great fireplace gothic in its details. But the furnishings and decorations are an entirely different matter. The hall is entered through a door in a wooden screen carved with classical arches and crowned by a renaissance balustrade. Above, there is a minstrel's gallery, though this is now divided into two. The vault is adorned with elaborate plasterwork containing medallions that depict Joshua with helmet and lance, King David with his harp, Hector of Troy and Alexander the Great. They surround a central pendant, on either side of which are displayed the arms of Danzig Willie and of his wife

Marjorie Woodward, daughter of a Provost of Edinburgh. William's heraldry is identified by the letters MWF, signifying that he was a Master of Arts of Edinburgh University.

Merchant though he was, he did not belong to the newly emerging class of town burgesses who were founding fortunes for themselves out of trade. He was a cultured aristocrat, reared in a castle before he built one for himself, and his great hall proclaims the fact. Its centrepiece, symbol of his status as a tenant-in-chief of the Crown exercising a capital jurisdiction, has earned these words from Douglas Simpson: 'The tremendous achievement of the Royal Arms of the United Kingdom over the hall fireplace is certainly the finest thing of its kind in Scotland, and may well have few equals in Great Britain.' It is placed between caryatids that support the plaster arch above. The lion of Scotland enjoys pride of place in the first and fourth quarters, while the devices of England and Ireland occupy the other two. The Orders of the Thistle and the Garter surround the shield. The crest above the sovereign's helmet is that of Scotland.

The smaller wing on this floor contains the withdrawing-room, whose flat ceiling is decorated with a design in plaster resembling those of formal gardens in this age, and dated 1625. But the most interesting feature of the withdrawing-room is the wall panelling of Memel pine. Timber was one of the most lucrative commodities that Danzig Willie imported, and Memel on the Baltic was the chief port to which logs floated downriver out of the forests of Russia, to be sawn into planks and traded.

One of the pine wall panels is a disguised door which leads through the thick wall to a tiny room beyond. This is situated in the square angle tower, above the entrance. There is space for a similar little room on every floor. In most other castles of this period, the angle tower was round, and contained the main circular staircase. It was one of the achievements of John Bell that he found space for his stairs elsewhere. There are never less than two stairways to each floor. A narrow circular stair leads from the kitchen to one end of the great hall while the main ascent leads to its entrance beneath the minstrel's gallery.

The little room in the angle tower is by no means so accessible. In addition to the hidden door in the panelling, there used to be a second at the farther end of the thick wall. It is hard to resist the conclusion that this was Danzig Willie's private office and strong room, especially as it is situated behind the fire of the great hall, so that it gave protection from damp to valuable documents. That other merchant prince of this age, Sir George Bruce, possessed a little room with precisely the same amenities, constructed for him at Culross Palace only a few decades before Craigievar Castle was built. So it is exceedingly curious that family tradition defines this one as the Prophet's room, and insists that it was not Danzig Willie's office but a chamber in which ministers were accommodated on their pastoral visits. They might have expected less cramped hospitality.

The broad straight stair to the hall landing gives way to a spiral one to the floor above. Here there is only space for one bedroom over the withdrawing-room and its dressing room above the Prophet's chamber, for the high vault of the hall occupies the longer wing at this level. It is not until a second flight of granite stairs has been climbed that the principal bedroom is reached. It contains a sumptuous bed reconstructed from one brought from the Netherlands in the seventeenth century, a plasterwork ceiling resembling that of the withdrawing-room and panelling in the same style, some of which was installed in the nineteenth century.

On this floor there is space at last for two bedrooms, and in the anteroom between them is a box bed, occupied of old by some senior matron of the household, within easy call of those she served. There are two box beds on a higher floor which are supposed to have held four younger maidservants. Down and up they went, by their separate spiral staircases, until finally these reached the long gallery at the top of the building. Still there were two more staircases, which gave access to separate platforms above the conical caps and gables of the roof, commanding a view of the approaches to the castle, of the pleasant valley through which the Leochel burn runs and, far to the north, of the summit of Bennachie.

Danzig Willie lived to see the completion of his delightful home before he died in 1627. By this time the need for such a place of strength must have appeared to be past. The union of the English and Scottish crowns in 1603 had removed the likelihood of future conflict between the two kingdoms. James VI avoided entanglement in the Thirty Years War that broke out in Europe in 1618, although it had begun with the deposition of his daughter, the Winter Queen of Bohemia, and her husband. Charles I likewise steered clear of the conflict when he succeeded in 1625. He did, however, permit his subjects to enlist in it as mercenary soldiers, and Danzig Willie's younger brother Arthur was among the many Scots who entered this alternative field of enterprise as the opportunities of commerce were blighted by warfare.

But presently there was fresh scope at home, with King Charles's attempt to introduce a liturgy resembling that of the Church of England in his northern kingdom. A National Covenant of protest was drawn up in Edinburgh in 1638, precipitating the great rebellion. It proved providential that Danzig Willie had built a stout castle after all.

His brother Patrick of Corse Castle, Bishop of Aberdeen, opposed the new liturgy, but he died in 1635 before the storm broke. His heir Professor John, despite his religious convictions, opposed the Covenanters when they took up arms against the King. They confiscated his property and drove him into exile. There, in Amsterdam in 1646, he published his great work on the Reformed Church which had such a widespread influence. Copies of his massive volumes are preserved at Craigievar.

The son of Arthur the soldier espoused the royalist cause, which proved fortunate when he was created Earl of Granard after the Restoration. Danzig Willie's son William, by contrast, fought for the army of the Covenant, for all that he had been created a Baronet of Nova Scotia by King Charles.

William had received a timely intimation of the gradual breakdown of law and order, reminiscent of an earlier age. Out of the hills to the west came a band of cattle thieves under a leader named Gilderoy, who did much damage to the estates of Corse and Craigievar until they were caught in 1636 and hanged in Edinburgh. Their heads were cut off and 'set up in exemplary places'. Four years later Sir William raised his first troop of horse in the name of the Covenant.

The danger to his cause and property increased alarmingly when Montrose arrived in Scotland to lead the royalist forces. In April 1644 William had 'his haill victuals' transported from the property of Fintray to the safety of his castle. Later during that year he fought in the first Battle of Aberdeen, when he had his horse shot under him and was taken prisoner. He regained his liberty by breaking his parole 'to the no small prejudice to his reputation'. Taking the field again at the second Battle of Aberdeen in 1646, he was captured once more. Meanwhile his cousin, Arthur's son, was fighting gallantly under Montrose.

But the King's cause was lost in Scotland by the autumn, and then Sir William was appointed Sheriff of Aberdeenshire. He died in 1648 and is commemorated by one of the George Jamesone portraits in the castle. His heir, John, was only twelve years old, which perhaps saved him from a fatal pitfall during the changes that occurred between the death of Charles I and the Restoration of his son.

There are two portraits of the second Baronet in the castle, each depicting the colour of hair that caused him to be known as the Red Sir John. He added several heraldic plaques to the plaster ceilings of passages and stairs with the date 1668, his initials, and his personal motto, 'Do not vaiken sleiping dogs.' The animals in his arms which somewhat resemble dogs are in fact the muzzled heads of bears.

Sir John lived into the reign of Queen Anne, and had the satisfaction of acquiring his ancestral estate of Corse from the son of Professor John, with its castle and its family portraits. These were removed to Craigievar while the old castle was allowed to fall into ruin until today only its foundations remain.

Red Sir John married Margaret Young of Auldbar who made the wall hangings which give the blue bedroom its name. This room is on the fourth floor, high enough to possess bulging alcoves where the corner turrets sprout from the corners of the tower. In these are shot holes covering the approaches, disguised by grotesque masks on the outside walls. Between the alcoves is a small window from which a Gordon is said to have been flung to his death, at some unspecified date and in circumstances that are not clear.

The Gordons, a Lowland family planted in the north-east at a relatively late date, became a thorn in the flesh of their longer established neighbours, and not least of the Forbes clan. The Gordon ghost continued to haunt the castle for as long as its Forbes owners lived in it.

It was the fourth Baronet, grandson of Red Sir John and Margaret his wife, who stood aside so discreetly during the 1745 uprising. Duncan Forbes of Culloden did more than any Scot to secure its defeat. Lord Forbes of Pitsligo raised a troop of horse to fight for the Pretender, and as a result his castle is a ruin today. Bishop Forbes was locked up in time to keep him out of danger, and after the defeat of Culloden he collected the tales of the Jacobites that were published under the title of *The Lyon in Mourning*. As in the wars of the Covenant a century earlier, the Forbes clan was as divided as others, except that the Laird of Craigievar remained sensibly neutral on this occasion. So Sir Arthur, fourth Baronet, preserved this jewel of the castles of Mar intact and earned his place in its portrait gallery.

His heir made the first marriage of this branch into the nobility when Sarah, daughter of the thirteenth Lord Sempill, became his wife. The portraits of this pair, painted by Sir Henry Raeburn, hang above the fireplace in the grand bedroom, known as the Queen's room although none of the three queens known to have visited the castle at different times actually spent the night here.

And now an event occurred, as it was bound to do in the end, that was apt to have a profound effect on such properties as this, for better or worse. The son of the fifth Baronet and Sarah Sempill succeeded to the estate but he produced no heir. So instead of an heir apparent there was merely an heir presumptive, a brother whose right of inheritance was only a contingent one. Such people usually found a form of livelihood which would support them in any circumstances. Being of the same generation as the incumbent, they had generally been allowed sufficient time to prosper before they succeeded to their patrimony. So it was in this case, and it occurred at a fortunate moment.

The childless sixth Baronet died in 1823. His brother and heir had served as a judge in India, from where he returned to find his home in a serious state of delapidation, and happily he possessed the means to remedy this. More providential still, he sought and heeded the advice of the distinguished Aberdeen architect John Smith, who wrote to him: 'The castle is well worth being preserved as it is one of the finest specimens in the country of the age and style in which it was built.' Under Smith's direction, it was repaired without the least alteration to John Bell's original work. It was even re-roofed in 1826 with Memel pine, on which were laid slates from the same quarries of Foudland that had provided the original ones.

But the plasterwork of the long gallery at the top of the building had evidently been damaged beyond repair by the leaking roof, and this room was divided in due course into servants' quarters and laundry premises. Although it has now been restored to its original proportions, it remains the sole disappointment of Craigievar. Here, in earlier times, the courts would have been held on occasion, judges and accused ascending by separate stairways at either end. Two bound manuscript court books remain on the gallery shelves, containing judgments that bring everyday life here in the early eighteenth century vividly to life.

Two examples must suffice. A man who set fire to his neighbour's door and called his wife and mother witches was fined £100 Scots.

Another, for wounding, drawing blood and destroying the peace of the district, was ordered to remove himself from the bounds of Craigievar and Corse within seven days, taking all his property, his wife and his children with him.

Apart from its gallery, the only other casualty to the building was the barmkin, or walled courtyard, that encircled the entrance and contained stables and other functional outhouses. This can be seen in a plan of the Mains of Craigievar drawn in 1776, but only a portion of the curtain wall remains today, with an iron-studded door bearing the initials of Red Sir John, and an angle tower beyond.

Instead of commissioning John Smith to modernise the castle for his convenience, the former Indian judge who was now the seventh Baronet instructed him to build a second home, a spacious mansion of granite, at Fintray twenty-five miles away. Here he could live in comfort with his wife Charlotte, daughter of the seventeenth Lord Forbes. Through this alliance with a member of another family holding an ancient Scottish title, capable of passing through the female line, the house of Craigievar doubled its chances of becoming elevated to the peerage by an accident of descent. It was the barony of Sempill, as it happened, that fell into the lap of the eighth Baronet.

Another fortunate accident ensured the survival of Craigievar. By the time its owner succeeded in 1884 as the seventeenth Baron Sempill, there was no longer a commodious Sempill mansion or castle to pass with the title. Otherwise the family might have moved to it, leaving the castle of Craigievar to share the fate of Corse. It was possible, nevertheless, that they might have embellished their home in a manner that reflected their more exalted status. This was an age in which such improvements were being carried out everywhere. Castle Fraser, which bears John Bell's inscription, is far from the most lamentable example of this.

But the seventeenth Lord Sempill had inherited Fintray House, as well as his father the former Indian judge's excellent example. From his time until the castle passed into the custody of the National Trust for Scotland in 1963, it was preserved as Danzig Willie had left it. The family continued to cherish it, dividing their time between here and Fintray. In the nineteenth century they installed modern plumbing without making any visible alterations except that water tanks were installed in the turret alcoves of the night nursery on the top floor below the long gallery. They did without electricity to the last. When a bath was installed in the twentieth century, it was concealed within the box bed in which a servant had slept outside the grand bedroom known as the Queen's room.

So it was that John Dunbar of the Royal Commission on Ancient Monuments for Scotland was able to write in 1966: 'At Craigievar, perhaps more readily than anywhere else in a country whose finest buildings are now often empty shells of studiously preserved masonry, it is possible to see a castle as its original occupants saw it.' Only one of these would have sufficed, in the course of three and a half centuries, to undo the work of preservation achieved by the others. Anybody who visits Craigievar today can see what a compelling temptation this must have been. Climbing its six floors by those steep, narrow spiral staircases, they may well wonder that elderly members of the family did not instal a lift. The thought of moving in that labyrinth in the dark, with nothing but a candle, might fill anyone with aghast admiration for its occupants.

Sir Ewan Forbes, the eleventh Baronet of Craigievar, is a grandson of the man who became Lord Sempill in 1884. Sir Ewan's elder brother succeeded to this title, and died in 1965, leaving a daughter to succeed as the Baroness Sempill, while the baronetcy and its property descended to her uncle of the male line. Consequently Sir Ewan is the last of his name to have been brought up in the home of his ancestor Danzig Willie. In 1984 he published a book called *The Aul' Days* which preserves a precious picture of his family life when it was divided between the castle and Fintray House.

It was affected by wide generation gaps. Sir Ewan's grandfather fought, before he was twenty years old, in the Crimean War that broke out in 1854. The bed in which he slept during that campaign is preserved in the castle. When the 1914–18 war broke out, Sir Ewan's father commanded the 8th Battalion Black Watch until he was severely wounded and invalided out of the army. Sir Ewan was only twenty years old when his father died, but old enough to have been influenced by a family tradition of exceptional interest. As he relates in *The Aul' Days*, his father was 'very particular about proper Scottish upbringing as taught by his father, with an insistence on being able to speak, read and write the Doric so that Scottish literature and verse could be fully enjoyed, and having a close understanding with all true residents of the land. He considered that inability to do so displayed apathy and ignorance of our race.' Sir Ewan's mother, who was Welsh, also learnt Doric with enthusiasm, 'and even endeavoured to

teach those in ignorance of the language a few practical sentences. I
remember one – "Dinna dicht yer nib wi yon cloutie." '

Hers was a more necessary accomplishment in the old paternalistic
days, when the vernacular was more widely spoken. 'My mother took
her part in the welfare of the estate's employees and tenant farmers
very seriously, and had a typed list for Craigievar of about sixty
holdings, and the same for Fintray, with names and addresses and a
column in which she marked down the date she visited them, at least
once a year and sometimes many more if there was illness. She would
get a lift to the furthest point she intended to call that day and walked
four or five miles home.' Sometimes she would send her little son with
supplies to the needy, and he thus acquired an early intimacy with the
folk among whom he was later to spend much of his life as a physician
when he was the heir presumptive to Craigievar.

The family flitting from Fintray to the castle took place early in
August. Two days in advance, the head housemaid made the twenty-
five mile journey on a bicycle, to prepare the beds with the local
caretaker's wife. On the morning of the move, Lady Sempill set out in
a governess cart drawn by a Shetland pony which she drove herself,
breaking her journey at the home of the Grants of Monymusk. She
was accompanied by Sir Ewan's sister, driving another cart drawn by
a Sheltie, and himself mounted on a riding pony. Even in those days
they must have presented a bizarre spectacle on the country roads.

For by now there were cars, and the family possessed two. One of
these followed later, driven by the chauffeur, bringing all the remaining servants except the butler. He travelled with Lord Sempill in his
Essex, with the family silver and remaining luggage. In those days the
long gallery was still divided into servants' quarters, and on one
occasion its roof drooped above the butler's bed. A local joiner cut
open the ceiling, and was drenched with honey from a heavy beehive.

As a rule the family returned to Fintray for the winter, but Sir Ewan
recalls the drought of the year 1921 which caused them to remain at
Craigievar, because Fintray always suffered from an inadequate
water supply. It was on those grounds that the fine house designed by
John Smith was demolished after the Second World War and its
contents largely dispersed, to Sir Ewan's great sorrow. He also
remembers an episode that is not included in his book, though it is not
a youthful memory that anyone would be likely to forget.

It happened that he was alone in the castle with his mother, taking a
bath in the box bed while she was in the blue bedroom on the floor

above. Hearing her footsteps as she descended the spiral staircase, he assumed that she was on the way to the entrance hall to collect the newspaper that was left there. He called out that he would bring it to her as soon as he could dry himself, wrapped himself in his towel, and took the candle which was his only light within the box bed bathroom.

By its flickering light he descended the stairway, a sufficiently hazardous course by daylight. There was always the risk that the candle would blow out; and woe betide anyone who dropped wax on the rough granite steps. He reached the ground floor and found neither his mother nor the newspaper there. The housekeeper had locked the door and retired to her house on the slope beyond the barmkin wall. Lady Sempill and her son were confined to the castle until she should return to unlock the castle in the morning.

Sir Ewan climbed the four floors to his mother's room, where he found her in bed, reading the newspaper. She had not left her bed. What Sir Ewan had heard was apparently the Gordon ghost, attempting to make a getaway down the stairs, rather than through the window of the haunted room in which Lady Sempill contentedly lay. Perhaps the apparition will be seen by others, now that the descendants of Danzig Willie live here no longer. Sir Ewan's personal flag still flies above the castle roof, and bees still make their hives in its secret recesses over the long gallery.

FYVIE

Among the uplands to the north-east of the Gramplans, where Aberdeenshire thrusts its broad peninsula into the North Sea, the castle of Fyvie stands beside the upper waters of the river Ythan. Here there was a royal hunting forest in ancient days, and here the Scottish kings established a strong fortress in the thirteenth century as a headquarters of local administration. William the Lion was here in about 1211 and his son Alexander II a decade later. Robert the Bruce dispensed justice at Fyvie after he had won the crown.

By his time the castle consisted of four square towers connected by curtain walls twenty-five feet high with a gatehouse in one of them, enclosing a quadrangular courtyard. A model of it has been placed on display in the building, and beside it another which shows how the present castle rises from the remains of the gatehouse front, and the wing that ran at right angles from its left side. The other two wings have disappeared entirely, with the corner tower that connected them.

In 1390 King Robert III granted the property to Sir Henry Preston, who had captured Sir Ralph Percy at the battle of Otterburn six years earlier. Such prizes were among the profitable perquisites of mediaeval warfare, and King Robert was in effect trading Fyvie for the ransom money.

It may have been Sir Henry Preston who heightened the walls and towers of his castle, enlarged the gatehouse and built a new dwelling against the curtain wall. But during the previous century Thomas the Rhymer had prophesied that Fyvie would not pass to an eldest son. Preston possessed no son at all, and it was his younger daughter who inherited, the wife of Alexander Meldrum of Meldrum, some ten miles to the south. His elder daughter made a second marriage to Sir John Forbes of Tolquhon, whose castle was another spectacular example of the Scots baronial castles of Mar, although a ruin today. It was to take nearly five hundred years for this senior branch to bear fruit at Fyvie.

The Meldrums were in possession of Fyvie from 1433 until they were compelled by financial embarrassment to sell the property in 1596. The part they may have played in heightening the corner towers and the premises added to the curtain wall, known as the palace range, is at present under expert investigation as the fabric is gradually stripped of its harling, examined and repaired. It was to be the new owner who transformed Fyvie into what Christopher Hartley has described as 'possibly the grandest example of baronial architecture in Scotland'.

He was Alexander, a younger son of the fifth Lord Seton, that devoted supporter of Mary Queen of Scots whose sister was one of the four 'Queen's Maries'. Alexander was described at his death as 'a great humanist in prose and verse, Greek and Latin, and well versed in the mathematics and great skill in architecture'. His erudition must have recommended him to Mary's son James VI, who raised him to the peerage first as Lord Fyvie, then Earl of Dunfermline. He placed his younger son Prince Charles in Seton's charge as his guardian, so that the boy who became heir to the throne on his elder brother's death spent a part of his youth at Fyvie.

Seton's transformation of the south front which contained the mediaeval gatehouse has been described by Richard Emerson as 'without precedent in the canon of Scottish tower houses'. The entire range between the two end towers was raised to a height of four storeys, using red sandstone and a coat of harling that concealed its difference from the earlier work on which it rested. The skyline became a fantasy of round turrets with conical caps, projecting from the topmost corners of the towers. Between these were dormer windows, one of which bears the date 1599, suggesting that this entire undertaking may have been completed in three years from the date of Alexander Seton's purchase.

One of its most arresting features is the oversailing arch that connects the two central drum towers which now soared above the entrance where the mediaeval gatehouse had been. This architectural device was to be copied elsewhere, notably in the nineteenth-century reconstruction of Blair Castle. The question is, who invented it in the first place.

Seton was remembered for his own 'great skill in architecture', but he possessed a close associate in William Schaw, the King's Master of Works, who died in 1602 and was buried in Dunfermline abbey. Here, one of his two epitaphs reads: 'Live in Heaven and Live Forever, thou best of men. To thee this life was toil, death was deep repose. In honour of his true hearted friend, William Schaw. Alexander Seton, Earl of Dunfermline.'

Unfortunately no certain evidence remains of the fruits of Schaw's life of toil, but John Gifford is among the experts who favour his claim to be the architect of Scotland's most remarkable castle front. Unlike the designer of Craigievar, Schaw left no other identifiable work with which to compare it. Perhaps evidence will one day come to light, authenticating William Schaw's contribution to Fyvie.

The other architectural wonder of the castle, its great circular stairway, is also without parallel. There is only one other in Scotland with which it might be compared, the smaller one at Noltland Castle in Orkney. Douglas Simpson demonstrated that the Noltland stairway was added to the building sometime after 1592, at about the time when Fyvie stairway was constructed, but there is no reason to suppose William Schaw had anything to do with it, even though he was the King's Master of Works and Noltland belonged for a time to the King's cousin Patrick Stewart, Earl of Orkney.

The Fyvie stairway was placed at the far, north-east end of the wing that extended from the great south front. It has a radius of ten feet as it circles round its central column, and it rises not merely to the main floor containing the great hall, but up to the floor above. The Seton coat-of-arms carved in the stonework faces the visitor at every turn. The marvel of this turnpike stair increases our sense of loss that so little else remains of Alexander Seton's new interior of Fyvie.

Amongst all that has been swept away is a painted chamber and two galleries, which survive only in a written reference. At the head of the stair a wooden panel has come to rest, carved with the inscription: 'Alexander Seton Lord Fyvie – Dame Gressel Leslie Lady Fyvie 1603.' Where it belonged originally is as much of a mystery as the original setting of panelling in what became the charter room, decorated with the crescents of the Seton heraldry, and two doors at the head of the stair bearing the same device.

The reference which provides such tantalising information is a contract of 1683, by which the fifth Earl of Dunfermline commissioned an Edinburgh plasterer to undertake decorations conforming to the Baroque taste of the time. 'Robert Whyte obliges him to plaster the Great Hall of Fyvie and dining room within the same, together with the great room above the said dining room above the said hall commonly called My Lady's Chamber, and closet within the same with handsome architrave frieze and cornice. Together with a painted chamber, Bed chamber, Lady Ann Erskine's chamber, Middle chamber, Wardrobe chamber, and the two low gallery chambers.

Together the whole closet and studies belonging to each of the said chambers with handsome plain cornice work.'

This is the most detailed description that remains of the Setons' home, and it introduces us to the earliest identifiable individual who worked at the castle. His ceiling survives in what was once the great hall, later converted into a morning room. So does the plaster ceiling at the top of the turnpike stair, and other plaster-work in a room on the third floor. It suffices to show that Robert Whyte was not in the front rank of Baroque plasterers of the age, although competent enough.

He had completed his task only a short while before the Setons lost Fyvie, forced to flee in 1690, as a result of their loyalty to James VII in the revolution which placed his son-in-law William of Orange on the throne. Thereafter the castle remained Crown property for decades in which it is likely to have suffered from neglect.

Finally it was sold in 1733 to the second Earl of Aberdeen, who owned the nearby estate of Haddo. Two years earlier he had commissioned William Adam to replace his old castle there with the handsome Palladian mansion that is now in the custody of the National Trust for Scotland, and he required a second home while the demolition and construction were in progress. But there was an entirely different reason also why he wished to add to his ancestral property. This was bound to pass to the heir by his first marriage, and he had made another to the Duke of Gordon's daughter. His bride was nineteen, he thirty years older, so that he might leave a relatively young widow homeless with their children unless he made timely provision for them. In the event, he died in 1745 leaving his son William Gordon heir to Fyvie at the age of nine.

William Gordon of Fyvie is immortalized by the most celebrated painting in the castle, arguably the finest portrait ever executed by the Italian artist Pompeo Batoni, of all the British notables who came to his studio. William rose to the rank of General, but when he posed for Batoni in 1766 he was still a Colonel. He is depicted wearing a kilt and voluminous plaid of the Huntly tartan.

It is supposed that William Gordon began his improvements to Fyvie some ten years after the visit to Italy commemorated by the Batoni portrait. This would seem to be attested by an armorial stone bearing his initials and the date 1777. Like earlier inscriptions of the Setons, it has been moved from its original position. The alterations were still in progress on the publication of Sir John Sinclair's Statistical Account of this area in 1793, which states: 'When the addition, which is at present making to the house, is finished it will be one of the largest and most commodious houses in the country.'

One of the steps General Gordon took to make his home more commodious was to enlarge the south range without altering its appearance from the front, in order to provide corridors for the bedrooms within. Previously, one room had led to another, as was usual in older houses.

But his most conspicuous addition to Fyvie is what is known as the Gordon tower. A plan that William Adam made for his father the Earl of Aberdeen, soon after he had purchased the property, shows that ruined vaults still remained of the quadrangular mediaeval castle, on the two sides not occupied by later buildings. Two of its corner towers were incorporated by now in the south front, while Seton's turnpike stair stood at the end of the wing which stopped short of where there had been a third tower. This is where Gordon placed his new one, beyond the great stairway.

He designed it to match the older end towers of the south front, showing a remarkably sympathetic respect for the work of earlier architects. Richard Emerson has words of praise for it on other grounds also. 'This determined and largely successful attempt to repeat the old work is, even for a date in the 1790s, an astonishingly early essay in the Baronial Revival.'

While it presented a similar appearance from the front to the other towers, it was deeper in its proportions, providing for a new kitchen on the ground floor with a dining room above. On the next floor there was a morning room, its walls green. Gordon's drawing room remained the former great hall, with Whyte's plasterwork ceiling.

The surroundings of the castle when he succeeded in 1745 consisted of three fields enclosed by forestry. By 1796 he had created a loch into which the burns ran, draining the swampy ground, which he transformed into parklands. Professor A. A. Tait suggests that he may have employed the landscape gardener Robert Robinson, who carried out similar improvements at Glamis some decades earlier. Gordon commissioned a walled garden, then a nursery garden beyond it. He planted trees, and created woodland walks in the Den of Rothie. The policies of Fyvie had been transformed by the time of his death in 1816, when he was succeeded by his son William, legitimised by his father long after his birth *per subsequentem matrimoniam*.

The second William Gordon of Fyvie left a rather puzzling description of the estate as he inherited it, in a statement attached to his will in 1844. 'The Castle of Fyvie in the year 1816 was, with the exception of a few apartments, in a state of delapidation, the farm offices were nearly ruinous, and there was a great deficiency of the necessary accommodation for a resident proprietor.' Perhaps he intended to suggest that his father had been too often an absentee, as a professional soldier, while there was no lady of the house. Or the General may have grown neglectful in his old age, for he was over eighty when he died.

The criticisms in his son's will extended to the surroundings. 'The low ground around the castle was one continuous swamp, and to the extent of at least 70 acres, totally unproductive. To remedy this the course of the river was changed and a new course also formed for the Skeugh Burn and drainage to a great extent carried on; by which operations 70 acres of the finest land in the parish have been added to the home farm. As a specimen of the extent of these operations, it may be noted that a new channel for the Ythan was made above and below, and through the Castle grounds to an extent little short of three miles.' Whether or not the second William Gordon was claiming the credit for what had been done by his father, the estate was certainly much improved.

Gordon had himself painted by Sir William Beechey on inheriting Fyvie, in the dress of a landed proprietor of the Regency era, very different from the flamboyant costume in which his father had posed for Batoni. Its sober elegance would have won the approval of that arbiter of taste, Beau Brummell. Gordon was forty-three years old when this very large picture was made, which hangs today on the turnpike stair. Its subject was no more a family man than his father had been: he lived for another thirty years without marrying.

He indulged many other interests, building an observatory and adding books to the library. His only contribution to the outside of the building was an entrance behind the Gordon tower and the great staircase, forming a long gallery with mirrors at either end to provide a reflection into infinity.

What paintings he added to the castle collection is uncertain, but the local landscapes of James Giles must have been his. Giles was an Aberdonian who first visited Fyvie when he was nineteen years old and soon formed a personal friendship with its laird, who introduced him to other patrons. His watercolours of the Balmoral estate helped to influence Queen Victoria to purchase that estate. In the year of

Gordon's death Giles presented a self-portrait to his patron, depicting him when he was forty-five years old and still remarkably handsome.

James Giles also painted for him a Virgin and St John, which fortifies a suspicion that Gordon may have become a Catholic. This could also account for the portrait of Prince Charles Edward in the castle, as well as the rare and precious miniature of Charles Leslie the Aberdonian ballad singer. Leslie had been born in 1677 and lived for a hundred and five years. This portrait of him was made two years before his death. So he had been a youth when James VII lost his throne, and had been able to compose and deliver his Jacobite songs into an age in which the Forty-Five was a distant memory. Apart from the evidence of these pictures, it is known that priests from the seminary of Blairs on Deeside used to visit Fyvie.

James Giles was not only an artist. He branched out into landscape gardening and played a major part in transforming Haddo into a model estate for the fourth Earl of Aberdeen, who became Prime Minister in 1852. It can scarcely be doubted that he was active also in continuing General Gordon's improvements to the estate of Fyvie, which his son made such large claims to have originated himself. Whatever the truth of this, there is no evidence of further work after the second William Gordon died in 1847 and was succeeded by a collateral.

It was Captain Cosmo Gordon who treated the old carved wooden panelling of the Setons with such disrespect, using some of it to decorate the charter room when he designed it as a smoking room, and other fragments to embellish the oak room at the head of the great stairway. Faced with the threat of a spendthrift cousin as his heir, he drew up papers to disinherit him, which he took to his solicitors in Aberdeen. Here he was so incompetent as to drop dead on the steps of his bank before he had signed them.

So Sir Maurice Gordon succeeded to Fyvie, where he made an oratory in one of the drum towers which the Earl of Dunfermline had planted above the mediaeval gatehouse. He also attempted to break into a walled-up chamber on the ground floor of one of the corner towers, hoping to discover hidden riches. Disappointed, he placed the property, including the castle and all its contents, on the market in 1885. So began one of the strangest stories in the history of any of Scotland's castles.

It was purchased by Alexander Leith, whose father Admiral John

Leith was a younger son of General Alexander Leith-Hay of Leith Hall, a scion of the lairds of New Leslie. But what mattered more to Alexander Leith was that his mother Margaret Forbes was the heiress of the nearby estate of Blackford, and descended from the house of Tolquhon into which Sir Henry Preston's elder daughter had married. Through her, he was heir to the senior line of the hero of Otterburn, on whom Robert III had bestowed Fyvie Castle in 1390.

According to a family tradition, this had been impressed on him at an early age. When he was no more than six years old, in 1853, he walked from Blackford to Fyvie and knocked on the castle door. Captain Cosmo Gordon was the proprietor when the servant opened it to ask him his business, and the child replied that he had come to inspect the property he intended to possess one day. The future of Fyvie might have been very different if he had determined instead to set himself up in the castle of Tolquhon, which might have been his only option if Captain Cosmo had not dropped dead on the steps of his bank.

Alexander Leith followed his father into the Royal Navy and was a Lieutenant in HMS *Zealous* when the ship docked at San Francisco in 1870. There he attended a ball, at which he met Louise, daughter of Derrick January of St Louis. The pair married in the following year, and Alexander Leith resigned his commission to join his father-in-law's Steel Company of Illinois.

In 1885 he was President of the company, and by a series of mergers he had soon made himself the controller of the largest company in the world. By the time the estate of Fyvie was offered for sale, he was well able to afford its purchase price and all he spent on the castle in addition.

He added an extension, designed by John Bryce, to the Gordon tower beyond the great staircase. This destroyed the effect achieved by General Gordon when he matched it so carefully with the older towers of the south front. The Leith wing has oriel windows decorated with the new proprietor's initials and those of his wife and the date 1890. Bryce derived these features from the nearby castle of Huntly, where they had been introduced at about the time when Seton was building his south front at Fyvie.

The kitchen on the ground floor of the Gordon tower was converted into a billiard room. In order to provide an entrance to it from one end of the Regency vestibule built by the second William Gordon, most of the mirrors had to be removed, which destroyed the original effect. On the other hand, the attention of the visitor could be focused with less distraction on the relief which depicted the heroic Sir Henry Preston in the battle of Otterburn, facing him as he entered. The dates 1390 and 1890 emphasised, here as elsewhere, that his descendant had recovered the property after five hundred years.

General Gordon's dining room on the floor above the kitchen was given a great panelled fireplace somewhat resembling the altarpieces in Baroque churches, framing a religious painting. This one surrounds a portrait of Louise January, with the bright quarterings of her husband's coat-of-arms amongst the carved woodwork above. An elaborate plaster ceiling with pendant bosses is likewise encrusted with his heraldry. From the opposite end of the newly decorated dining room Alexander Forbes-Leith (for he had adopted his mother's surname) surveys the scene, dressed in a kilt of the Forbes tartan.

If this was drastic, it was nothing to what occurred on the floor above, the level at which the oriel windows sprout from Forbes-Leith's extension to the Gordon tower. Here he decreed a music room, serving also as a ballroom, as an annexe to General Gordon's morning room, now converted into a drawing room. These two connecting rooms constitute the *tour de force* of Forbes-Leith's contribution to the castle, and one of the most sumptuous interiors of the Victorian and Edwardian age in the hands of the National Trust for Scotland.

Above the end oriel window a great organ was installed in 1906, purchased from Herbert Marshall in London. It is supported on a balcony whose screen is made up of fragments, probably from the decorative woodwork of Dutch churches. Tapestries line the walls, round an impressive chimneypiece. At the end of the drawing room, the kilted Colonel William Gordon averts his eyes to contemplate the laurel wreath in the hand of a marble effigy of the goddess Roma.

There is more from which he might have averted his eyes in other parts of his former home. His drawing room, once the great hall, did not lose its seventeenth century plaster ceiling in favour of more Forbes-Leith escutcheons, but it became a morning room, with new panelling and fireplace. The small drawing room behind it was refashioned as a picture gallery. But although Forbes-Leith has been criticised for his somewhat ruthless treatment of an ancient and historic building, posterity owes him much for preserving it. He might have built himself instead a palace in the pleasant climate of Florida or California.

But his religion was ancestor-worship, and this drew him home: and with all his outstanding personal gifts, he proclaimed that the social status and accomplishments of his forebears were at least as important to him. He acquired all the family portraits on which he could lay his hands, as though asserting that unlike the other self-made millionaires of his day, the Pierpont Morgans, the Fricks and the Guinnesses, he was an aristocrat by descent. His relatives seem to have been remarkably complaisant about parting with their portraits, and so he was able to build up a collection which is one of the glories of Fyvie. For by good fortune Forbes-Leith not only possessed distinguished ancestors, but ones who had been painted by outstanding artists.

So Fyvie not only possesses the finest single collection of Raeburns, but also the completest set of likenesses of that outstanding dynasty of scholars and scientists, the Gregorys. Here is James Gregory, born in 1638, who distinguished himself at the universities of Aberdeen and Edinburgh, Padua and Oxford, and who invented the reflecting telescope. It was John Scougal who painted his portrait. He married a daughter of George Jamesone the artist, who is to be seen here with his wife and one of his children. Well might Forbes-Leith be proud of such forebears as these.

The astronomer's grandson John Gregory became Physician to the King in Scotland, and married a daughter of Lord Forbes. John Cotes painted her in 1756 and her husband in 1764, and here their portraits hang. The astronomer's great-grandson James became Professor of Medicine at Aberdeen University and sat to Sir Henry Raeburn. He made a comparatively late marriage to young Isabella MacLeod of Geanies in 1796, and Raeburn celebrated the event with a portrait of her that has been hailed as his finest work. In the same year he depicted a totally contrasting subject, a cousin of James Gregory within a few weeks of his death. His name was Thomas Reid, and his mother was Margaret Gregory, married to the Minister of Strachan. Reid was Professor of Philosophy at Aberdeen and published his influential *Inquiry into the Human Mind* in 1764.

One of the most touching Raeburns at Fyvie is the portrait of John Stirling of Kippendavie, who raised thirteen children, so that he was elderly when his youngest daughter was growing up. She nestles against him in Raeburn's study of affection between young and old.

106

Forbes-Leith did not descend from the lairds of Kippendavie, but his sister was married to one of John Stirling's descendants.

But the Raeburn collection would not be the best there is in any one place if Forbes-Leith had not widened his net beyond the family circle. Thus, he added the full length portrait of Sir William Maxwell of Calderwood, standing beside his horse, for its intrinsic merits. He purchased other pictures because their subjects were Scots, particularly if they belonged to the north-east.

Raeburn was the one Scottish artist of his time who enjoyed a celebrity comparable with that of Gainsborough and Reynolds, Romney and Hoppner. Forbes-Leith collected portraits by these others, only sometimes with a Scottish connection. There is Romney's picture of Captain Arthur Forbes of Culloden, by no means a near kinsman. In the case of the Lawrence portrait of Susanna, Countess of Oxford, he has settled for a masterpiece in this study of the wealthy dowager with her dog in her lap.

Happily Forbes-Leith was able to remind himself of the career of his great-uncle Captain Andrew Forbes, Commander of HMS *Thracian* when her guns were thrown overboard during a hurricane off North Carolina. The painting by William Huggins of this event is only one of several that recall the family's long association with the Royal Navy. There is de Gruyter's painting of the destruction of the Spanish Armada, van Minderhout's study of the humiliating capture of the *Royal Prince* by the Dutch in 1666, and Hoppner's Admiral Nelson, painted after the battle of Copenhagen in 1801.

Forbes-Leith only once bought a Turner, and he resold it. He was not interested in such *avant garde* artists as Cézanne and Gauguin. He preferred Sir John Millais' scene of the river near Dunkeld. A mystery that remains is, how many of the pictures at Fyvie were already in the castle before the Gordons sold it. One might suppose that these include the portrait of the beautiful Duchess Jane, wife of the fourth Duke of Gordon, who is also to be seen in Brodie Castle. This picture is a copy by Raeburn of the painting of Sir Joshua Reynolds. It was the Duchess Jane who played such an eccentric part in the recruitment campaign when the 100th Gordon Highlanders were raised in 1794, holding the silver shilling between her teeth so that the men who joined the Colour virtually kissed her on the lips. It was Forbes-Leith who acquired this portrait of her, and also the Raeburn portrait of her son the fifth Duke of Gordon.

He was created Lord Leith in 1905. By then his only son had died on active service in the Boer War, so he was succeeded at his death in 1925 by his daughter Ethel Louise, the wife of Sir Charles Burn, a Baronet and Member of Parliament. Her portrait by Sir Luke Fildes in the castle depicts a striking woman who displayed her father's gift for organisation when she helped to run the nursing services during the First World War. She and her husband changed their names to Forbes-Leith under the terms of her father's will, bringing themselves within range of Thomas the Rhymer's prophecy that no eldest son would succeed to Fyvie. It was their second son who did so, and his second son Sir Andrew who followed him. Sir Andrew sold Fyvie to the National Trust for Scotland in 1984, but took the muniments with him, which have not been made available to those who are trying to establish the provenance of the castle's contents and the successive periods when it was built. Many mysteries remain locked in those documents while the patient exploration of the castle's stonework continues.

THIRLESTANE

The towers and turrets of Thirlestane sprout from their rock above Leader Water as though they were a natural growth. To the south, this tributary joins the Tweed in the Debateable Land. To the north, the Pass of Lauderdale leads to Edinburgh. The castle occupies a site which has been of strategic importance from time immemorial. Before the Romans came, Welsh-speaking Britons lived here and their inscriptions can be seen in the Border Country Life Museum that has been created in the courtyard wing of Thirlestane Castle.

After the legions had left, Angles who had settled on the rock of Bamburgh in the fifth century advanced north to conquer and colonise. The people they encountered were known to the Romans as the Votadini, the latinised form of the Welsh Gododdin. When the Gododdin counter-attacked, marching as far south as Catterick, they were utterly defeated. The Angles then colonised Lauderdale, but in the eleventh century a new sort of overlord arrived in Britain. The ancestors of the Maitlands crossed from France to England with William the Conqueror in 1066, and after the premier Baron of England had inherited the Scottish crown in 1124 as King David I, they were among the members of their feudal order who came to settle in these northern pastures. Whatever fortification occupied the rock of Lauder when they arrived, it was not they who strengthened it initially, but King Edward of England. In 1296 he embarked on the conquest of Scotland, and such places of strength as this were fortified throughout the land as the seats of his military garrisons. As soon as King Robert the Bruce was able, he dismantled them, so that the mediaeval castle on the rock of Lauder belongs to a later age.

But here it stood when Sir William Maitland died on the field of Flodden with his king in 1513, leaving as his heir the distinguished lawyer and poet Sir Richard Maitland. The family's principal seats at this time were Lethington Castle near Haddington, later known as Lennoxlove, and Thirlestane, which stands about two miles from the fort of Lauder. Sir Richard is remembered as the author of the *Solace of Age*, and for his priceless collection of the works of earlier Scots poets. This is no longer to be seen in Thirlestane Castle. It was purchased by Samuel Pepys about a century after it was made and is preserved in his library at Magdalene College, Cambridge. But the portraits of Sir Richard's two remarkable sons hang here.

William Maitland of Lethington, the elder of them, acted as Secretary of State both to the Regent Mary of Lorraine and to her daughter Mary Queen of Scots, and remained loyal to Queen Mary's cause until 1571, when he and Kirkcaldy of Grange were forced to surrender Edinburgh Castle. His son died without issue, and it is from his younger brother John that the Maitlands of Thirlestane descend. John became James VI's Chancellor and is perhaps best remembered for the part he played in placing the 'Golden Act' on the statute book, which has been called also the Magna Carta of the Church of Scotland.

It was John Maitland who, between 1570 and 1590, enlarged and modernised the fort of Lauder as his home, moving into it from nearby Thirlestane and bringing the name with him. In 1590 he became a Peer of Parliament as Lord Maitland of Thirlestane.

In transforming Lauder fort into his castle of Thirlestane, John Maitland may well have been inspired by Lethington, the tower house in which he had been brought up, though his elder brother had inherited it; and by their poet-father's encomium on his home.

> *Thy tower and fortress, large and long,*
> *Thy neighbours does excel;*
> *And for thy wallis thick and strong*
> *Thou greatly bears the bell.*
> *Thy groundis deep and topis high*
> *Uprising in the air,*
> *Thy vaultis pleasing are to see,*
> *They are so great and fair.*

Maitland of Thirlestane, too, made a fortress large and long, opening windows in mediaeval walls up to thirteen feet in thickness. They can be seen in a room that was re-panelled in the nineteenth century, and which contains portraits of the poet's two sons. The elongated building terminates in two round corner towers, their top floors corbelled out to carry square chambers with crow-stepped gable roofs. From the north and south sides of the castle smaller towers bulge, in a complex served by no less than eleven spiral staircases.

Maitland's heir married Isabel Seton, daughter of the Earl of Dunfermline who was enlarging Fyvie Castle at about the same time. In 1624 she became a Countess when her husband was created Earl of Lauderdale a year before the death of James VI. Dying in 1645, he was spared the hazards that followed the defeat of Charles I in the great civil war, and fortunately he left an heir who was both astute and lucky enough to survive until the restoration of Charles II in 1660, with his castle intact. It still contains the coronation robe in which the second Earl attended that ceremony.

He was to prove the outstanding member, if not the most likeable, of a family rich and versatile in its talents. He became one of the ministry called the Cabal after the initial letters of its members' names, the last of which represents Lauderdale. By subtle manoeuvres he ousted all his rivals until he became known as the King of Scotland. He displayed considerable statesmanship in steering his course between rival religious and political factions, and it was during his rule that Scots law became established firmly, codified by distinguished jurists. He was besides a scholar and a bibliophile, and when he transformed Thirlestane from a castle into a palace he commissioned the greatest architect his country had ever reared, William Bruce.

Bruce was an aristocrat like himself, related to the Earls of Elgin and Kincardine. He had been at least as active as Lauderdale in negotiating the restoration of Charles II. The two men were cultured amateurs: Bruce received no formal training in architecture, though he was a travelled man with an informed and observant eye. King Charles appointed Bruce Superintendent and Overseer of the royal palaces and castles in Scotland, and Holyroodhouse remains his most famous achievement. The home he built for himself at Kinross has been called 'the most beautiful and regular piece of architecture in Scotland'. Its designer was described as Scotland's Inigo Jones and Christopher Wren rolled into one. Among castles, Thirlestane is his masterpiece.

A third person played a dominant part in this achievement, Elizabeth Murray, Countess of Dysart in her own right, and heiress of Ham House by the Thames near London. She had married Sir Lyonel Tollemache in 1647 and had a son. Lauderdale was married to the Earl of Home's daughter but had no male heir. It appears that Bessie Dysart and Lauderdale began their liaison long before either was widowed, she having an insatiable lust for power as well as the necessary charm to trap men in her web, while Lauderdale wielded the power she craved.

Bishop Burnet, a scion of the family who owned the castle of

Crathes on Deeside until it passed to the National Trust for Scotland, attested that she 'had a wonderful quickness of apprehension, and an amazing vivacity in conversation; had studied not only divinity and history, but mathematics and philosophy; but what ruined these accomplishments, she was restless in her ambition, profuse in her expense, and of a most ravenous coveteousness; nor was there anything she stuck at to compass her end'. Successive portraits by Sir Peter Lely depict the progressive hardening of her cold, ruthless eyes. Only one of these hangs in Thirlestane, but others may be seen at Ham House, which was presented to the English National Trust on most generous terms by its Tollemache owner in 1948.

After Bessie Dysart's husband died, she had to wait another two years for the Countess of Lauderdale to do the same. By then she was forty-five years old, Lauderdale over ten years her senior. However, as Bishop Burnet recorded, 'Lady Dysart had such an ascendant over his affections that neither her age, nor his affairs, nor yet the clamour of his friends and the people, more urgent than both of these, could divert him from marrying her within six weeks of his Lady's decease.' As for the effect on him, Burnet said that he 'had acted with much steadfastness and uniformity before, but at this time there happened a great alteration in his temper, occasioned by the humours of a profuse, imperious woman.'

Charles II celebrated the union by creating them a Duke and Duchess: the Letters Patent of this advance in the nobility may be seen in Thirlestane Castle. Evidently this hardly sufficed the Duchess who, according to Burnet, conducted herself 'with a haughtiness that would have been shocking in a queen'. She was punished in savage lampoons, which compared her with the mistresses of Charles II.

> *Since the King did permit her to come to Whitehall*
> *She outviews Cleveland, Portsmouth, young Fraser, and all.*

The Duke shared in the obloquy.

> *She's Bessie of the Church and Bessie of the State,*
> *She plots with her tail, and her lord with his pate.*

These, then, were the pair who transformed Thirlestane, until it was very much as we see it today, directing Sir William Bruce, cousin of the Duchess through her Bruce mother. It was in 1672 that the Lauderdales were married. By the April of 1673 the Duke was thanking Bruce for 'the plans and perspectives of my three houses'.

112

(He had commissioned work on his home of Brunstane in Midlothian and Lethington near Haddington, as well as Thirlestane.) The ground before the west end of the old castle of Thirlestane was lowered, so that a flight of stairs could rise to a new entrance beyond a paved court, enclosed by a pavilion on either hand. In this way the building became T shaped, Bruce's front forming the top of the T. 'I am glad the avenue is so hard and it is planted,' Lauderdale told Bruce; 'but I am sure the mason work will not be so soon finished. For you may remember that I was very positive to have the two pavilions next the house raised one storey higher.'

It was Bruce who introduced classical renaissance architecture into Scotland, replacing the vernacular style of Scots baronial. William Adam, builder of the Palladian house of Haddo and father of the Adam brothers, worked under him. So did the King's Master Mason Robert Mylne, whose family was to make such a notable contribution to Inveraray in the next century. The stature of Bruce is to be seen in his influence as well as his buildings.

At Thirlestane his art takes an altogether novel form. The doorway beyond the elegant flight of stairs and the paved court is of the Doric order. But above it rise corbelled arches, defensive towers and high corner turrets. Here we have a precurser of the baronial revival of a later age, though reduced to a symmetry such as the Bell family never dreamed of imposing on the castles of Mar.

Work had already begun on Holyroodhouse before Bruce was drawn to Thirlestane, and both men and materials were purloined from the royal palace to serve the Lauderdales. It appears that Thirlestane also swallowed up public funds, for as the Duke conceded, 'This I know will cost money, but without it I shall never endure the front of my house, and therefore of necessity it must presently be done.' He was referring to the need to heighten the pavilions on either side of the new entrance.

There is a strong presumption that the Duchess would not have endured it either. She had inherited at Ham a Jacobean house that she was determined to transform into the most sumptuous mansion of the age in England; in this she succeeded. While Lauderdale continued to rule Scotland for another six years after his marriage, his time and his purse were poured into the creation of almost Ruritanian filmsets in England and Scotland, in which he and his domineering wife could hold court with regal splendour.

How far the internal decorations are to be attributed to the taste of

Sir William Bruce is a matter of surmise. His own plaster ceilings, like those of Holyroodhouse, do not attempt to compete with the flamboyant ostentation of those of Thirlestane and are no less pleasing on that account. Charles II's two favourite plasterers, George Dunsterfield and John Halbert, had been sent to decorate his palace in Edinburgh, from where they presently found themselves deflected to Thirlestane.

Here their work is astonishing in its virtuosity. Indeed, there is nothing else to compare with it in Scotland. The staterooms on the upper floor of the old castle had occupied the entire width from wall to wall, forming a succession of apartments that opened one from another. From the ante-room at one end to the Duke's private closet at the other, the King's English plasterers decorated the ceilings in a manner designed to create increasing wonder as suppliants and courtiers sought to make their way from one end to the other, where they might hope to reach the ducal ear.

All this plasterwork took John Dunsterfield and his assistants over five years to complete, and it reached its climax of splendour in the large drawing room. Laurel leaves give way to garlands of flowers and fruit. There are clusters of musical instruments. The eagles which form the supporters of the Lauderdale coat-of-arms occupy corner panels. An extraordinary effect is created by the plaster wreaths of oak and laurel which hang suspended from the ceiling, drawn as though by the force of gravity. The Duke's inner sanctum contains his coronet in each corner of the ceiling and his crest in the centre.

Two Dutch craftsmen added their skills. At Ham they had renovated the windows among other services, and been described as 'most excellent workmen, both at that trade and for making cabinets'. It was they who panelled the ante-room through which visitors hoped to pass, to reach the presence of the great Duke. The hopeful suppliants would enter and leave through doorways such as are not to be seen anywhere else in Scotland, doorcases consisting of classical columns that support swan pediments, such as the royalty of central Europe favoured.

This incomparable display of power, wealth and corruption in high places was achieved at Thirlestane less than two decades after the rule of Cromwell, when Lauderdale had been imprisoned under sentence of death for his support of King Charles before his defeat at Worcester in 1651. It was rumoured that Bessie Dysart had been the mistress of the Protector, improbable as that may seem, and had therefore been able to secure Lauderdale's release. Cromwell had given both England and Scotland the most just and efficient administration they had ever enjoyed, creating the beginnings of a civil service staffed by 'very honest clerks' and 'men who made some conscience of what they did'.

It was hardly a democratic process which restored the kind of regime exemplified by the Lauderdales, but it appears to have been generally popular – for a time. Now that the will of the public is expressed effectively through the ballot box, exactly the same trends occur as replaced the austere Rule of the Saints with the one that the Lauderdales celebrated at Thirlestane. But eventually King Charles responded to the mounting clamour, in Parliament and beyond its walls, and deprived the Duke of all his offices in 1680. Lauderdale begged the King not to allow his 'old and faithful servant to die in poverty', but Charles was too astute to compromise himself in the unpopularity of a minister.

Perhaps Lauderdale's temper had been undermined by a painful kidney disease, from which he died in 1682. His behaviour must have been affected by the *folie de grandeur* of his wife, encouraging as it did a tendency of his own. Indeed it is strange that these two well-born Scots, who were so cultivated and intelligent, contrived at the same time to be so vulgar, contributing that flashy element to the decorations of Thirlestane which is absent from the other work of Sir William Bruce.

The furnishings do not speak of the lifestyle of the Lauderdales with the same eloquence. It is at Ham House in Richmond that these are preserved in an altogether exceptionally complete form. The Duchess knew that her husband's property would pass to his brother at his death, apart from the provision for his daugher and the extinction of his ducal title. Ham House would descend to her eldest son with the earldom of Dysart, so to Ham she despatched fourteen wagon-loads of furniture from Thirlestane. Only one of these was stopped by the enraged people of Lauder and sent back to the castle.

So it is that there are all those Maitland portraits in the house that John Evelyn described in 1678 as 'furnished like a great Prince's'. The Duchess continued to live at Ham until her death in 1698, sixteen years after that of her husband. During that time there was a danger that Thirlestane would fare worse still, when the fourth Earl of Lauderdale remained loyal to James VII in the revolution of 1688.

But he died in exile without issue and the family home passed unscathed to his brother.

Despite the loss of the portraits to Ham, Thirlestane preserves one of the finest portrait collections to be seen in any such home in Scotland. Here are Secretary Lethington and his brother Chancellor Maitland of Thirlestane. The latter's son the first Earl is delineated here by George Jamesone. Seven paintings by John Scougal preserve the features of subsequent members of the family. Portraits of the Duke were executed by Sir Peter Lely, but Scougal depicted his brother the third Earl, his wife, his daughter Mary, his son the Jacobite fourth Earl, the younger son who became fifth Earl, and two other sons. It is an exceptionally rich collection of Scougal's art.

The most fashionable artist in Scotland at this time was Sir John Medina, and it was he who contributed the portrait of the fifth Earl's wife Margaret, only child of the tenth Earl of Glencairn.

To Medina's studio came William Aikman, who had been born in Forfarshire in 1682, the year of the Duke's death. He was to become a member of the distinguished circle which included the poets Allan Ramsay and James Thomson, as well as men of letters outside Scotland such as Alexander Pope and Dean Swift. Aikman added the sixth Earl to the gallery, son of Glencairn's only daughter, together with his wife and two of their sons. The sixth Earl left eight sons and two daughters in all when he died in 1744 after serving as President of the Police and High Sheriff of the County of Edinburgh.

He narrowly missed the arrival of the Young Pretender, which would have been an embarrassment to him in the offices he held. It was left to his son the seventh Earl, who inherited those offices, to accommodate the Prince in October 1745, after his victory at Prestonpans, on the eve of his fatal march into England. The room in which Prince Charles Edward slept was the one in which the Duke's brother and heir had been born, but the bed in it today belongs to the Regency period. Some fifty years after the death of the thieving Duchess, the castle was still so bare of furnishings that it was necessary to borrow the bed in which the Prince slept from the nearby town of Lauder.

From this time onwards prosperity increased as members of the family fulfilled their traditional role of resident patriarchs of a country estate in the age of improvement. Younger sons and heirs who had not yet inherited took commissions in the armed services, and we can see their likenesses still together with those of their wives, executed by Reynolds and Hoppner, Romney, Lawrence and others. Some of them rose to high rank. One younger son, born in 1771, became an Admiral, and so did the tenth Earl, born in 1786. It was to Captain Sir Frederick Maitland that Napoleon surrendered aboard HMS *Bellerophon* after his defeat at Waterloo in 1815. He is commemorated by a bust in the great drawing room, where items of his crockery are also preserved.

In the army there was Lieutenant Colonel John Maitland, a hero of the American War of Independence (in British eyes), and Lieutenant General Sir Thomas Maitland, a younger son of the seventh Earl, who became Commander of the Forces in the Mediterranean. The tradition of army service continued until the fifteenth Earl's heir was killed in action in 1943, so that Thirlestane passed eventually to his daughter's son Captain Gerald Maitland-Carew.

Among earlier members of the family is the Whig statesman Charles James Fox. His marble bust is displayed in the entrance hall, his gaze fixed, beneath bushy eyebrows, on the improvements made to the castle after his death. They belong to the 1840s and were carried out by the same team of architects – William Burn, David Bryce and his nephew John Bryce – who ministered to this fashion also at Brodie, Blair, Fyvie and elsewhere.

Here they extended Sir William Bruce's front by adding matching pavilions beyond those of the architect royal. Although they resemble the original ones they are distinguishable by their darker stonework. Perhaps they were not improved by the oriel windows inserted on the second storey of the old and new pavilions alike. But an imaginative addition was made when the towers enclosing the entrance beyond the court were given flat roofs with balustrades, and the central tower above the doorway was heightened and crowned with an ogee roof, that is, one containing a double curve.

Within, the hall in which Charles James Fox's bust stands was given a new plaster ceiling in 1840, a great deal more restrained in its design than the earlier ones in the staterooms above. So too is that of the dining room placed by Burns and Bryce in one of the added wings. Unlike those of Fyvie, it is not festooned with heraldry proclaiming the distinguished alliances of the Maitland family. There is no need. This is where as many of the incomparable collection of family portraits as the walls will hold is placed on display, the Duke in the place of honour over the mantelpiece.

It was the creation of this new room in 1840 which enabled the architects to convert the old dining room into the larger library. Many of the Duke's precious collection of books had been sold, like the manuscripts of the old Scots poets which Samuel Pepys bought. But some remained and others had been added. Above the bookshelves may be seen the porcelain collection which J. J. Bell-Irving brought from China in about 1900, beneath a new plaster ceiling in the same restrained good taste as that of the entrance hall. A painting of Bell-Irving's beautiful wife is preserved in the castle also, with her young daughters, one of whom married the fifteenth Earl of Lauderdale.

The enlargement of their home in Victorian times was not motivated by a need for display. Improved travel facilities led to greater mobility in an upper class that was closely inter-related. Medical science had diminished infant mortality and cured diseases that carried off adults. Noble families would visit one another with their large families of children, and bringing their own servants. Thirlestane itself was staffed by about forty living-in servants up to the time of the fifteenth Earl and additional bedrooms and nurseries had to be found to provide for the round of visits. So it was that apart from the great dining room in the new south wing of the castle, the nineteenth-century additions served an entirely functional purpose, while the dining room itself was required merely to seat more guests, not for purposes of ostentation.

This way of life, which had been destroyed at a blow in the French revolution of 1789 and in the Russian revolution of 1917, became eroded in Britain by a process of peaceful change which has preserved intact much of our national heritage that might otherwise have perished. Former owners have been transformed into custodians and trustees, and this is what has occurred at Thirlestane.

When Captain Maitland-Carew succeeded to his grandfather's former home in 1972, he was thirty years old. The structure of the ancient building had deteriorated dangerously and it was entirely beyond his means to undertake the necessary repairs. There were forty different cases of dry rot, while the central tower added by Bryce to Sir William Bruce's front was in danger of falling down. He travelled the country speaking to many different Trusts and people including the Secretary of State for Scotland. In 1977, the Historic Buildings Council for Scotland were persuaded to start on a series of substantial grants towards a major rescue operation lasting until 1987.

Above Thirlestane Castle; *below* The Large Drawing Room

1st Duke of Lauderdale by Sir Peter Lely

Above View of Floors Castle (1809) by William Wilson; *below* The Castle today

Above The Drawing Room; *below* Duchess May, wife of 8th Duke of Roxburghe

The Ballroom

Dunrobin Castle

Above The Drawing Room
Below The Library

William, 18th Earl of Sutherland by Allan Ramsay

In 1984 Captain Maitland-Carew realized that, even with revenue from visitors, he could not continue to finance the on-going maintenance on this huge building. He appealed to the National Heritage Memorial Fund. The problem was solved when he gifted the main part of the castle with its contents to a charitable trust. The National Heritage Memorial Fund then endowed the charitable trust so that the castle could be properly maintained for the foreseeable future. The Maitland-Carews continue to own and occupy the north wing of the castle and a member of the family will continue to be a trustee.

The happy solution that has been found is different from that by which Brodie of Brodie handed his castle to the National Trust for Scotland on such generous terms, or that by which the Trust was enabled by grants of public money to acquire Fyvie Castle from its owner, with as much of its contents as he was willing to surrender. It is different again from that of Glamis, Blair, Floors and Inveraray, where the owners have opened their homes as local and national amenities, run on a commercial basis.

Meanwhile a different kind of activity began at Thirlestane in 1982 when the Border Country Life Museum Trust leased the courtyard wing of the castle and began in the following year to adapt it to their purposes. As at Culzean Castle, they have received support from many other public bodies: the Borders Regional Council, the Countryside Commission, the Manpower Services Commission and the Scottish Tourist Board. The story of Border life is being carefully pieced together here.

Here are the souvenirs of the Romans and a grave-find earlier still. Here prehistoric settlements, disclosed by aerial photography, can be traced once more beneath later field systems. All sorts of tools of the past have been gathered in the steading, from saws to veterinary appliances and medicines. The life of the gamekeeper is illustrated by displays of the game and the predators that he reared and trapped. A limekiln and tileworks have been reconstructed, a reminder of the time when limestone was quarried both for building and as a fertiliser. The photographs of all kinds of farmers and craftsmen recall the centuries in which Thirlestane and its owners were the heads of a sort of corporation, the source of employment for miles around and of the well-being of hundreds, if not thousands, of people.

There is a display of horse traction, harness and traps, as well as a reconstructed tailor's shop. A cobbler and saddler's shop, plus an old smithy, are being constructed. The Border Country Life Museum

Trust has now been taken over by Thirlestane Trust which has been most fortunate to have received on permanent loan from the Pollock Toy Museum some several thousand toys of the pre-plastic age which visitors can enjoy, on show in the old family nurseries. Downstairs, connecting the castle to the country life exhibitions, are the Victorian kitchen, scullery and laundries reconstructed as of bygone days. Local volunteers are glad to conduct visitors round the castle, as others are to contribute their skills to the burgeoning museum of Border life. Thus, while the young heirs of the Maitlands can still enjoy the castle in which their ancestors lived, so can everyone else whose forebears belonged to this great estate.

FLOORS

The windows of Floors look across the River Tweed, where it joins the Teviot as these frontier waters make their way to the sea at Berwick. Not far away the ruins of Kelso Abbey rise above the town, while the crumbling walls of Roxburghe Castle lie directly opposite, across the Tweed.

Nothing at Floors is so old. The entrance gates were erected in 1929. The turrets, cupolas and battlements beyond them swirl in the mists of the nineteenth century. Sir Walter Scott described these surroundings as a kingdom for Oberon and Titania, but he was dead before his own enchanted castle at Abbotsford was upstaged by this riot of fake English Tudor architecture. It is startling to recall that it was the creation of William Playfair, who played such a memorable part in transforming Edinburgh into the Athens of the North.

Born in London and trained in Glasgow, Playfair had built the Royal Scottish Academy in massive Doric in 1822, over a decade before he came to Floors. He had taken up the interrupted work on Robert Adam's university buildings, planted his Parthenon on Calton Hill, and laid out classical circuses and terraces in the new town. His other masterpieces in Greek revival style are the National Gallery and the Royal College of Surgeons. But even in Edinburgh he had flirted with neo-Tudor, and at Floors he was able to indulge his every whim in the extravaganza that is termed a Scottish castle today.

Of course it is not a real castle, and no castle ever stood on this site. There was a Georgian mansion, built here a century earlier by William Adam, and that is all. A painting by William Wilson preserves its original appearance, in the familiar view seen by motorists as they drive along the opposite bank of the River Tweed. Starting work in 1838, Playfair built pavilions on either side of it, enclosing a forecourt at its entrance. The eastern block was to provide the stables, while the western pavilion was designed to provide administrative offices.

By 1849 the Adam mansion itself had been transformed to conform to the rest of Playfair's creation. It contains three upper floors above a partly sunken basement, more or less as it appears in William Wilson's painting of 1809. But its flat roof is ornamented with globular finials rising at intervals from the wall-head, and the corner towers

121

are gabled and pedimented like the larger corner towers of the new pavilions on either hand. On the opposite side of the castle, which faces the River Tweed, there is a central loggia supporting a *perron*, a platform reached by external stairs. From this south-east aspect can be seen Playfair's ballroom added to one side of the old house, and the orielled extension to the dining room on the other.

From every angle this sprawling complex flaunts its embattled parapets, its pepper-pot turrets, its ornate water-spouts. They join the skyline and the tree-tops in a setting that was said to have been too large in scale for its former mansion. Playfair's castle would overflow less ample surroundings.

But Floors is something more than a flamboyant statement of the taste of an age, such as might have appealed to a parvenu millionaire industrialist. It would have been no less eligible to stand as a sample of the castles that sprouted in Scotland during the Victorian era if it had been built for Citizen Kane. But in fact it is the seat of the tenth Duke of Roxburghe, a representative of one of the most ancient and powerful clans of the Border country, the Kers. Their very real castles are scattered throughout this region. But every one of them has been abandoned by its owners, and whether ruinous or restored they no longer possess their original contents. Only at Floors are these open to public inspection today.

This will place the visitor in difficulty unless he directs his mind elsewhere during a sweep of action-packed centuries in which Floors was merely a parcel of church lands owned by the abbey of Kelso. The evidence for this is to be seen in the castle, the facsimile of a royal charter which added to the property of the Benedictine monks, of which the original is on loan to the National Library in Edinburgh. Its initial letter depicts King David I, who founded the abbey in 1128, and his pious grandson Malcolm IV who endowed it further.

The family who were to acquire these lands at the Reformation were described by the Lord Lyon, Sir James Balfour Paul, as 'of unquestioned Scandinavian origin,' their name identified with that of the man in the saga story about the voyages of Kari. Ker, Kerr and Carr are the most common variants among Scottish surnames. If this derivation is correct, then the Kers were part of the Scandinavian element in the Northumbrian kingdom which also contained Britons and Angles when Roxburghe Castle was built, a key stronghold in the Debateable Land.

It was ceded to King David I by the English, but it remained a bone of contention for years to come, until James II laid siege to it in 1460. He was killed by a huge gun called the Lion, which exploded in his face as he ignited its charge. The spot is marked by a post beside a tree in the grounds of Floors. His gallant widow Mary of Gueldres pressed on with the attack while her little son James III was hastily crowned in nearby Kelso Abbey. Once Roxburghe Castle had been stormed, it was razed to the ground.

The ancestors of the Dukes of Roxburghe were living at this time a short distance to the south, in Cessford Castle near the junction of the Tweed and Kale water. Their descendants might be living in it still, but for the bonanza of those abbey lands. John Ker of the Forest of Ettrick had acquired the lands of Altonburn in 1357, about the time when the oldest part of Cessford Castle was built, and his descendant Andrew Ker of Altonburn had obtained a formal title to it before James II was blown up by his cannon. It was either he or his son Walter who enlarged it into the massive L-shaped tower which the English esteemed as the most formidible stronghold in the area after the destruction of Roxburghe Castle. Today it is a ruin of red free-stone with lighter coloured dressings, some of its walls about fourteen feet thick, with fragments of a barmkin wall and surrounding earth-work.

But this was by no means the only seat of the Kers. Six miles from Kelso stands the peel tower of Smailholm, the most perfectly preserved in the Border country. This had belonged to the house of Altonburn at least since 1404, and in the reign of James III Andrew Ker of Cessford bestowed Smailholm on his second son Thomas.

Meanwhile the senior line of Altonburn possessed a third castle at Ferniehurst, built on a high bank above Jed Water, two miles from Jedburgh. Thomas of Smailholm married the heiress of Ferniehurst, and thus the two principal branches of the Kers ought to have preserved amity with one another, as well as consolidating their property within the clan. But they did not. By the time the sixteenth century opened there was bitter rivalry between them, threatening the destruction of both.

The conflict centred largely on the office of Warden of the Middle March of the Border with England. In 1502 Sir Andrew of Ferniehurst was appointed Warden, but after the death of James IV on the field of Flodden in 1513, Sir Andrew of Cessford received the office in the following circumstances.

James IV's widow, Margaret Tudor, made a second marriage with unseemly haste in 1514. Her husband was Archibald Douglas, Earl of Angus, and since the Kers of Cessford owed vital charters to the Douglases, Sir Andrew Ker of Cessford's allegiance to the Douglas party is understandable. It earned him the wardenship, but committed him to the pro-English lobby. On the other hand, Sir Andrew of Ferniehurst gravitated to the young King James V, who grew up with an understandable contempt for his mother and an irrational hatred for all Douglases. When the Earl of Angus was driven into exile, Cessford followed him to the court of Queen Margaret's brother, Henry VIII of England. Ferniehurst came into his own for a while.

In 1542 King Henry invaded Scotland and defeated James V at Solway Moss. James died soon afterwards, leaving the baby Mary Queen of Scots as his heir. Ferniehurst Castle was captured by the English and in 1545 the magnificent abbey of Kelso was reduced to a ruin in what became known as the Rough Wooing. It failed in its object of securing the hand of the little Queen Mary for King Henry's son, and the Scots were rescued with the help of the French.

An officer of France named Beaugué described the reprisals when Ferniehurst Castle was recaptured in 1549. The violation of women and other atrocities committed by the English had made Sir John Ker of Ferniehurst extremely eager to capture the enemy alive. 'I myself,' wrote Beaugué, 'sold them a prisoner for a small horse. They laid him down upon the ground, galloped over him with their lances at rest, and wounded him as they passed. When slain, they cut his body in pieces and bore the mangled gobbets in triumph on the points of their spears. I cannot greatly praise the Scots for this practice. But the truth is that the English tyrannized over the Borders in a most barbarous manner, and I think it was but fair to repay them, according to the proverb, in their own coin.'

The rivalry between Cessford and Ferniehurst continued during the troubled reign of Mary Queen of Scots. Cessford was a partisan of the pro-English faction which destroyed the Queen, and took part in the rout of Langside that drove her into England. Ferniehurst, by contrast, continued to support her cause for as long as there was any prospect of her restoration. He incurred the animosity of James VI, who ordered the destruction of his castle in 1593. But five years later its L-shaped tower was restored, and it still stands above Jed Water.

Meanwhile the rival branches of this militant clan found a more profitable field of enterprise when both espoused the Reformed Faith. Ferniehurst was one jump ahead, for Mark Ker became Abbot of Newbattle, and then Commendator when this title of office was substituted at the Reformation. After his death in 1584, his son Mark was created Lord Newbattle three years later. His family soon recovered the King's favour after the slighting of their castle, and in 1606 Mark was advanced to the rank of Earl of Lothian.

Newbattle was a Cistercian abbey founded by David I in 1140, and enlarged at intervals since then. Little but the foundations remain, for as Scotstarvet wrote, the Kers 'did so metamorphose the building that it cannot be known that ever it did belong to the Church, by reason of the fair new fabrick and stately edifices thereon.'

Inspired by the example of his senior cousins, Sir Robert Ker, younger of Cessford, abandoned his boisterous career in the Border country before he reached the age of thirty, to become a Privy Councillor in 1599. His father died in the following year, and by 1602 he was in possession of the abbey lands of Kelso with the rank of baron. He accompanied James VI to London when the King succeeded to the English throne, and was created Earl of Roxburghe by 1616. His portrait at Floors, the earliest of his family that hangs in the castle, is believed to have been executed by George Jamesone.

It brings us face to face with a man who had turned his back on the mediaeval past and its local preoccupations, to help lay the foundations of a new age. He was the last to live in the castle of Cessford, and he died at Floors, though before the present family home had been built there. He became an adherant of Maitland of Thirlestane, that astute statesman whose castle stood a few miles to the north, at the entrance to Lauderdale. He married a Maitland as his first wife, though she died leaving him with only one son who expired in his youth, and one daughter. He made a second marriage with Jean Drummond, whose portrait hangs at Floors beside his, and she gave him another son.

So he did not lack a male heir when the rebellion broke out against Charles I. He supported the King while his son joined the Covenanting opposition, but this provident arrangement was frustrated when his son died in 1642, leaving only daughters. The Earl of Roxburghe was now over seventy years old, his third wife childless. The dynast lost interest in the King's problems, to concentrate on his own. He provided that his title and property should devolve on his grandson by the daughter of his first wife.

This youth was instructed to marry his first cousin, the eldest daughter of the son of his second marriage. Dutifully he did so, and thus the succession continued by a double descent from the first Earl into the nineteenth century. One of the younger grand-daughters made an alliance with a member of one of the most ancient families of Moray, Sir James Innes, the twenty-second Chief of Clan Innes. This connection may have appeared at the time of little consequence to the future of Floors.

The Earl of Roxburghe died and was succeeded by his young grandson in 1650, the year in which Charles II arrived in Scotland to make a bid for his father's throne. The second Earl joined the Royalists, and was fined £6000 by Cromwell after their defeat. In 1658 his heir was born, whose portrait in Floors Castle, in rich Restoration costume, introduces us to the man endowed with a double strain of the Ker blood.

He became Earl on his father's death in 1675, but survived him by only seven years. In 1682 Charles II's brother and heir, James, Duke of York, sailed to Scotland where he had been appointed Lord High Commissioner. The twenty-four-year-old Earl of Roxburghe accompanied him in the frigate HMS *Gloucester*. His ship was wrecked off Yarmouth and he was drowned. But he left two sons, the elder of whom succeeded at the age of five, and lived to pose for the portrait that hangs at Floors before dying unmarried at the age of nineteen. Such were the accidents that help to explain the long interval of time between the abandonment of Cessford Castle and the building of the family home on its present site at Floors.

It was the younger of those two sons who finally embarked on this, after he had succeeded as the fifth Earl in 1696. He was described as 'a man of good sense, improved by so much reading and learning that he was perhaps the most accomplished young man of quality in Europe, and had such a charming way of expressing his thoughts that he pleased even those against whom he spoke.'

Prominent among these were the opponents of the incorporating Union with England, which created the United Kingdom of Great Britain in 1707, abolishing the Parliament of the Scots in Edinburgh. Roxburghe was among its eloquent supporters, and this earned him a dukedom. His very real abilities were also displayed in the office of Secretary of State for Scotland, and his courage when the Jacobite uprising of 1715 occurred and he joined the Duke of Argyll as a volunteer at the battle of Sheriffmuir.

Castles were long out of fashion when building commenced at Floors in 1721. It used to be thought that Vanburgh was the architect, but it is now generally agreed that William Adam both designed and built the house that forms the centrepiece of Playfair's castle. For a century it remained as he had devised it.

The second Duke succeeded to it in 1740 and died fifteen years later, leaving an only son who never married. He had become engaged to a Princess of the house of Mecklenburg-Strelitz, but when her younger sister married George III protocol forbade that an elder sister should become the subject of a younger, and so the betrothal was terminated. There are earlier and later portraits of the third Duke at Floors, by Gilbert Stuart and John Hoppner. Anyone might wonder, pausing to examine them, at the thoughts of a man whose life was ruined by such a preposterous rule of etiquette.

Evidently he made and kept a vow of celibacy, although by doing this he was risking the destruction of everything his forebears had created at Floors. He consoled himself with the pleasures of a bibliophile, and his priceless contribution to the treasures of this castle went under the hammer as a result of his failure to provide an heir. For there was a disputed succession after his death in 1804, and by the time it was resolved by the House of Lords in 1812, the collection had to be sold to meet the costs of the lawsuit. 'No sale of books ever engrossed a larger share of public attention,' remarked the *Gentleman's Magazine*.

The calendar of contents fills a volume entitled: 'A Catalogue of the Library of the late John Duke of Roxburghe arranged by G. and W. Nicol, booksellers to His Majesty, Pall Mall, which will be sold by auction at his Grace's Residence in St James's Square on Monday 18th May 1812.' Some of its items fetched astronomical prices, and a group of purchasers combined to form the Roxburghe Club, in commemoration of the sale of Valdarfer's edition of the *Decameron* of Boccaccio. They commissioned facsimiles to be made, so that the collection could be duplicated among them. In this way the life's work of the third Duke of Roxburghe was largely preserved by a handful of enlightened noblemen, whose use of their wealth contrasted admirably with that of certain others during the Regency era.

The fourth duke of Roxburghe succeeded to the title at an advanced age, and died within a few months. The succession of Sir James Innes as the fifth Duke had a curious consequence. He was the twenty-fifth Chief of Clan Innes, which had been recognised as a clan by the Privy Council in 1579, and his descendants enjoy that office to this day. On the other hand, they do not enjoy the chiefship of the name of Ker, which has descended in the male line through the Ferniehurst branch, whose head was raised to the rank of Marquess of Lothian by King William of Orange in 1701.

The fifth Duke of Roxburghe was seventy-six years old and childless when the House of Lords decided in his favour in 1812, so that there was a grave danger of another disputed succession at his death, involving further loss to the patrimony of Floors. But when he was over eighty years old his young wife presented a son to him, who became the sixth Duke at the age of seven. It was he who commissioned Playfair to transform his Georgian mansion into what is called a castle.

Externally, Floors remains almost exactly as Playfair left it, but the interior has since been altered; for Sir Henry Innes Ker, who succeeded as eighth Duke of Roxburghe in 1892, married Mary, daughter of the American millionaire Ogden Goelet. The Goelets kept a list of eligible young men: it contained as many heirs to dukedoms as possible, like the lists of other rich Americans. The Goelets triumphed over some of these when they installed their daughter in Floors, for which they were willing to pay a handsome price. The castle had to be altered to accommodate the property she brought with her.

Much of it had crossed the Atlantic to furnish her family home on Long Island, and dated from the reigns of Louis XIV, XV and XVI in France. The revolution there had led to sales; in the long run, the American revolution created a nation of buyers. The purchase of a coronet resulted in a second sea journey for the endowment of Duchess May, as she became known. She was particularly fond of tapestries, and the castle contains one that eclipses all the others. It hangs in the anteroom, a fifteenth-century panel woven in Brussels which depicts the descent of the Holy Spirit on the day of Pentecost. The lifelike expressions of the men and women receiving the gift of tongues, the colours and folds of their costumes, the gold thread, the intricate weaves which depict formal flowers as well as the faces in such detail, make this a captivating work of art. It alone is worth a visit to Floors.

Duchess May recreated the drawing room in the style of Louis XV to hold her Brussels tapestries of the seventeenth century: Neptune by the sea, Flora in her garden, the feast of Bacchus, Apollo and the Muses, Venus at Vulcan's forge. A Louis XV suite of gilt chairs contains Beauvais tapestry covers illustrating the fables of La Fontaine. There is a commode from Versailles, and cabinets of the reign of Louis XVI. In a corner hangs a small oval portrait by Kneller of the fourth Earl who died when he was nineteen, a reminder that we are neither in France nor in the Victoria and Albert Museum, but in the Border country of the Kers.

One of the tower rooms is thought to have been transformed by the Duchess May into a copy of another at Versailles, as a setting for more of her French furniture. The walls are lined and windows curtained in pink silk damask. Here is another Louis XVI suite of chairs covered with tapestry, a Louis XVI writing table, a Louis XV dressing table. One of the portraits of the Duchess hangs in this room, in the company of others by Hogarth and Allan Ramsay.

But it is Playfair's ballroom that was most radically altered, for it was redesigned to accommodate the great Gobelin tapestries of the reign of Louis XIV. Clocks, writing tables and other French furniture of the eighteenth century line its walls. Here, as elsewhere, there is also a great deal of Chinese porcelain. The walls are panelled with wood, their otherwise plain surface embellished with carvings in the style of Grinling Gibbons.

One such display of fruit and flowers surrounds a portrait of a young woman holding a lute, above a mantelshelf adorned with oriental objets d'art. This is Lady Margaret Hay, who presented three daughters to the first Earl of Roxburghe's son before his death in 1642, one of whom married Sir James Innes. It is intriguing to chance upon these earlier members of the family, peeping out from the corners to which they have been consigned by the American Duchess. The first Earl and his wife are also to be seen at the end of the ballroom, gazing on its strange medley of treasures from foreign parts.

There are stranger ones elsewhere, not least the umbrella handles made by Fabergé, which the Duchess could unscrew, enabling her to pick her handle for the occasion as a man might choose his tie. As for the family into which she married, her husband fought in the Boer War and was severely wounded in the Great War. Their son served in the Middle East during the 1939–45 war, and their grandson the present Duke only abandoned a military career in order to administer the enormous estate he has inherited.

Today the castle is open to the public, and it should be visited. But those who are interested in Border history and the part which the Kers played in it must not suppose that this is the most evocative place in which to seek either. There is the massive ruin of Cessford and the delicious tower of Smailholm, neither far away. Newbattle, converted from an abbey into a mansion, was given a battlemented top storey in 1886, during the final transformation carried out by William Burn and James Bryce. Finally the eleventh Marquess of Lothian presented it to the nation early in this century, as a residential college of adult education.

Ferniehurst, the ancient seat of the Ker chiefs, still preserves its tower, to which a wing containing a great hall was added in the seventeenth century. For half a century from 1928 it was used as a Youth Hostel, until the twelfth Marquess of Lothian undertook its repair with the assistance of the Historic Buildings Council. It was opened to the public in 1986, and remains the place of assembly for the Jethart Callant, when two hundred riders set out from Jedburgh on the second Friday in July, to be greeted at the castle by the Chief of the Kers, commemorating the bloody events described by Beaugué over four hundred years ago.

> *The castle, razed from tower to floor*
> *Was built and garrisoned once more;*
> *The Scots and French, led on by Kerr,*
> *Courageous and well-trained to war,*
> *On horse, on foot, from far and near,*
> *With Jethart axe and Border spear,*
> *Responded to the bugle-call.*

So wrote Walter Laidlaw, a former custodian of Jedburgh abbey, in the poem that is recited during the ceremony at Ferniehurst. This annual ritual, and the place where it is consummated, is the proper complement to the spectacle of Floors.

DUNROBIN

Like Floors, Dunrobin as it appears today is a mid-nineteenth century building whose architecture betrays foreign influence. While the inspiration of Floors is an English Tudor palace, that of Dunrobin is a French château. The difference is that there was never a castle at Floors. Encased in the modern stonework of Dunrobin are the remains of a very old castle indeed.

How old is impossible to say. It stands on the shore of what had been the Sutherland of the Vikings, looking across the Dornoch and Moray Firths towards the lands of Moray in the south. William, great-grandson of a Fleming named Freskin, was created the first Earl of Sutherland in about 1235, and it has been surmised that he descended in the female line from the royal house of Moray. Perhaps the earliest portions of the castle may date from his time, but the oldest surviving tower, with its iron yett, was built after 1400, while its name, Robin's Castle, is thought to derive from that of the sixth Earl, who died in 1427.

This, at any rate, is the dynasty from which sprang Clan Sutherland. To the north lies the Caithness peninsula, the territory of the Sinclairs. They had fallen heirs to the Norse earldom of Orkney when this still belonged to the Crown of Norway. After it had passed to the King of Scots in the fifteenth century, they were bought out of their island property and compensated with the earldom of Caithness.

West of Caithness lay the great province of Strathnaver, extending as far as Cape Wrath and down the west coast to Assynt. It was divided from Sutherland by a chain of hills, the *Crioch Ardain* or Frontier Heights. This was the homeland of Clan Mackay. Their Gaelic patronymic is *Aodh*, an ancient name of the kings of Moray, from whom they were reputed to descend in the male line.

Thus the mediaeval castle of Dunrobin was planted in the midst of a tribally based society, part Norse and part Gaelic and still using those two languages during the Middle Ages. But presently there arrived a very different folk, who had belonged to the southern Border of Scotland where the language of the Angles had been planted. These were the Gordons, whom King Robert Bruce planted in Strathbogie in Aberdeenshire, and who were created Earls of

131

Huntly in 1445. Before the century was out they had begun to implement their plans to take over the earldom of Sutherland, using the conventional means of eliminating the true owners, charges of idiocy, bastardy and criminal behaviour.

John the eighth Earl of Sutherland laid his family open to this when he gave his daughter Elizabeth in marriage to Adam Gordon, younger brother of the Earl of Huntly. Her mother was a daughter of the Lord of the Isles, who had already borne a son and heir, likewise named John, before she perished when the ferry that was carrying her across the Kyle of Sutherland capsized. Her husband then made a second marriage with the daughter of Alexander Ross of Balnagown Castle, a scarcely less prestigious alliance with a member of the ancient Gaelic aristocracy. The son of this marriage was named Alexander. Such were the *dramatis personae* in the drama about to unfold at Dunrobin.

The eighth Earl of Sutherland had entered into his inheritance in 1455, and had managed his affairs competently for over forty years through troubled times before the Gordons brought a brieve of idiocy against him. He died in 1508 without having suffered anything worse, and his wife was drawing her maintenance from the estate as the widowed Countess until at least 1512. Adam Gordon attempted to have his wife Elizabeth served heir in May 1509, but the elder of her two brothers was declared heir in July as ninth Earl. Her younger brother Alexander was induced to renounce his claim in the same month, which might have appeared a proper fraternal act until he discovered that a brieve of idiocy had been entered against the ninth Earl also. Thus Adam Gordon gained possession of the estate by right of his wife in 1512.

This was made easier through the vice-regal powers that had been bestowed on the Earl of Huntly as the King's Lieutenant in the north. Nevertheless the plot might not have succeeded but for the battle of Flodden that was fought in 1513. While so many of the Scottish nobility died, defending their King, the Earl of Huntly and his brother Adam Gordon fled the field, to bring their plot to fruition during the hiatus of authority that marked another royal minority. When and in what circumstances the ninth Earl died is uncertain, but on his death Alexander Sutherland became the legitimate heir, and his claim was advanced by the Sinclair Earl of Caithness and by Mackay of Strathnaver. The Gordons based their own claim on the improbable fiction that Alexander was illegitimate.

In 1518, during the absence of Adam Gordon, Alexander arrived at Dunrobin with forces brought by the Earl of Caithness and Mackay, and captured the castle in which he had been brought up. But the Gordons hastened to recapture this strategic bridgehead, on the route to more northern properties. After they had done so they captured Alexander Sutherland, placed his head on a spear, and planted it on the top of the castle tower. It was not until 1550 that his son John was able to make another attempt to recover Dunrobin. He was killed in the castle garden, but he left sons in his turn.

By the time this occurred both Adam Gordon and his wife Elizabeth, through whose title he had called himself Earl of Sutherland, were dead and had been succeeded by their grandson as the eleventh Earl. The enterprise had succeeded perfectly, and it was soon to be copied by others, the Mackenzies in their expropriation of the MacLeods of Lewis, and the Campbells in their takeover from the MacDonalds of Islay. An important difference in these two cases is that there was no peerage title among the assets.

The Reformation enabled the Gordons to acquire property deep in the heart of Caithness and Strathnaver, for the Diocese of Caithness, whose headquarters were Dornoch in Sutherland, comprehended both of these provinces. In 1541 Robert Stewart was appointed Bishop of Caithness at the age of nineteen, although neither then nor subsequently did he take Holy Orders. His sister married the eleventh Earl of Sutherland, to whom he conveyed extensive Church properties in 1553, seven years before Catholicism was abolished by Act of Parliament. They included those of Scrabster near Thurso in Caithness as well as of Dornoch itself: 'because the said castles of Scrabster and the palace of Dornoch are built in an Irish region, among fierce and unsubdued Scots'. Scrabster did not lie in a Gaelic region, though the church lands of Strathnaver did, which he also handed over to his brother-in-law the Earl.

He kept the Priory of St Andrews for himself, where he retired among his cronies 'who colluded with the revellers of the town to hold the ministry vacant, and in the meantime took up the stipend and spent the same at the golf, archery, good cheer'. He lived to see his sister's son succeed as the twelfth earl in 1567 at the age of fifteen and marry Jane Gordon, daughter of the Earl of Huntly.

Jane, Countess of Sutherland, is the earliest of the matriarchs of Dunrobin whose features are preserved in the castle. Those steady eyes had seen much. Her first husband had been the Earl of Bothwell, from whom she was divorced so that he could wed Mary Queen of Scots. In 1573 she was remarried to the Earl of Sutherland and she bore him three sons whose portraits are also at Dunrobin. She lived to witness many religious changes before her death in 1628, and the crucifix she holds in her picture attests that she never wavered in her faith. Her son Sir Alexander of Navidale also remained a devout Catholic, and fared the worse for it, in this world at least.

The children of the twelfth Earl and his wife were Gordons of both branches of the family, and none demonstrated the implications of this better than the son who became Sir Robert Gordon of Gordonstoun, and tutor to his nephew when he succeeded as fourteenth Earl, aged six, in 1615. The Gordon attitude he exemplified, stated in his own words, echoes that of his uncle the fun-loving Bishop who was condemned to spend some time attending to Church affairs among the 'unsubdued Scots'.

The Tutor of Sutherland, writing to his nephew, advised him to 'use your diligence to take away the relics of the Irish barbarity which as yet remains in your country, to wit, the Irish language and the habit'. The language he condemned as Irish was the original language of the Scots, but the Gordons believed it to be their mission to replace it by that of their place of origin, English. As for the habit, Highland dress, 'purge your country piece by piece of that uncivil kind of clothes'.

His uncle the sixth Earl of Huntly had proposed more thorough methods than these, a few decades earlier, when he undertook to exterminate all the Gaels of the isle of Lewis in 1605 and replace them by English-speaking Lowlanders. 'His Lordship offers to take in hand the settling the North Isles,' Huntly informed the government, 'and to put an end to that service by extirpation of the barbarous people of the Isles within the year.' The islanders were saved by Huntly's greed, when he haggled over the feu duties of the lands he set out to conquer for himself, and annoyed the King.

Sir Robert Gordon the Tutor recommended a more gradual form of expropriation. 'Be not too hard-handed to them at first, for by a little freeness and liberality you may gain them, which is the nature of all Highlanders. Yet by progress of time I wish you to send some of your own people to dwell amongst them.' The Gaels at the receiving end of these tactics were the Mackays of the great province of Strathnaver that lay beyond the mountains to the north of Sutherland.

Their Chiefs posed a threat which the Gordons had adopted a

radical measure to eliminate. The Catholic Countess Jane possessed a daughter of the same name who had been married to Mackay of Strathnaver and borne an heir. It was thus possible that a failure of male Gordon heirs might leave the succession to a Gaelic Chief, and that Dunrobin would cease to be an enclave of English civility in the midst of the Irish barbarity, or a strategic centre for Gordon enterprise. A new grant to the earldom had therefore been obtained in 1601, which limited the succession to the surname of Gordon in the male line. A consequence of this provision was that the earls could not aspire to be the chiefs of Clan Sutherland, which required that they should bear that name. Of course there remained the Sutherlands of the disinherited line, as there still do to this day.

The Mackay grandson of the Catholic Countess Jane was the Chief whom Charles I created Lord Reay in 1628, the year of his grandmother's death. 'The noble Sir Donald Mackay, Baron of Reay and Lord of Strathnaver' he was addressed by the Danish Chancery, after he had raised the Mackay Regiment to fight under Charles I's uncle Christian IV of Denmark in the Thirty Years' War. This undertaking ran him into debt, and he incurred further losses through his loyalty to King Charles in the great rebellion.

The Gordons bought up his debts, which gave them possession of the Naver valley from which Strathnaver takes its name. But by far the greater part of it, to the east and west of this valley, remained in possession of the Mackays until the nineteenth century. All the same, the Gordons now bestowed on themselves the title of Lord Strathnaver, although they never obtained letters patent from the Crown, the only source of any peerage title. Perhaps they might have wheedled such a grant out of Charles I at a time when he was scattering titles to right and left in an attempt to gain support. But they had deserted his cause with too much alacrity to qualify.

Lord Reay died in exile in 1649, a few weeks later than his King. In that same year the Earl of Sutherland obtained from Parliament the funds for a garrison of a hundred men to occupy the Mackay Chief's house at Tongue, his seat since the Gordons had destroyed his castle of Borve, some twelve miles along the coast to the east, in the previous century. Tongue house was demolished altogether before Charles II was restored in 1660, and the present building dates from after that time. But the return of the King saved the Mackay Country from the Gordons, although they retained the Naver valley and still consoled themselves with their bogus title of Lord Strathnaver.

The seventeenth century ended in greater harmony when both the Mackays of Strathnaver and the Gordons of Sutherland supported the Williamite revolution of 1688, and took the field on behalf of the Hanoverian succession in the Jacobite uprising of 1715. Boundary disputes continued in the debateable land until, only a fortnight before Prince Charles landed in Scotland in 1745, the third Lord Reay wrote to the seventeenth Earl of Sutherland, 'I heartily wish that all our differences were buried in oblivion.' So they were, in time for the two men to unite in opposition to the Jacobites.

After Prince Charles had retreated to Inverness early in 1746, the Jacobite Duke of Perth sailed up the Moray Firth and captured two ships off Dornoch carrying supplies for the Hanoverian forces of the far north. But the treasure chest eluded him, for it had been carried to a man of war standing out to sea. The Earl of Sutherland fled from Dunrobin by boat, taking with him the public money entrusted to his charge, and leaving his wife to entertain the Jacobites who moved into his castle. Thus he avoided the dangers of a siege.

On 15 April the Jacobite Mackenzie Earl of Cromartie arrived with three hundred men and his son Lord MacLeod. They were returning from the north, where they had failed to raise recruits owing to the efficient measures taken by the Mackays. According to one report, Cromartie and his officers were 'drinking and carousing' at Dunrobin while some of their troops were attempting to cross the ferry to the Dornoch peninsula a few miles to the south. Here they were set upon by Ensign John Mackay with a contingent of the Sutherland militia. After taking them prisoner, Ensign Mackay surprised the revellers in Dunrobin, and caught the Earl of Cromartie hiding under a bed. John Mackay was a tacksman of Mudale near the southern borders of Strathnaver, and a distinguished religious poet whose compositions were published in the nineteenth century. On the day after he broke into Dunrobin, pistol in hand, the Prince's army was destroyed at Culloden.

Dunrobin Castle ranks with Blair Castle as one of the last two in Britain to have been involved in military conflict. It can no longer be seen as it appeared at that time, because in the nineteenth century as much as was left standing of the ancient building was encased in a new castle that was built round it. But from the central well in the later structure can still be observed a portion of the circular tower from which it may be that the head of the disinherited Alexander Sutherland was displayed. It is attached to a square keep of lesser height of which a strip remains exposed.

An old picture reveals that a crow-step gabled block had been attached to the keep, somewhat like the one that was added at Culzean late in the seventeenth century. There were further additions containing corner towers, and a barmkin, an enclosure within a high wall such as so many tower houses possessed. This complex, perched on its height above the bay, bears a distinct resemblance to the one that faced Robert Adam when he came to Culzean, overlooking the waters of the Firth of Clyde.

In the eighteenth century the Gordon earls changed their surname to Sutherland, which may well indicate a change of attitude to the Gaelic peoples among whom they lived. Sir Robert of Gordonstoun's desire to see the Gaelic language obliterated had not been fulfilled. Instead it had become the vehicle for the most eloquent voice ever heard in Sutherland or Strathnaver, that of the poet Rob Donn Mackay (1714–78). Highland dress was indeed proscribed for disaffected and loyal clans alike but during the period of proscription the eighteenth Earl of Sutherland had himself painted in the kilt.

As for 'the Irish barbarity' of 'the unsubdued Scots', which the Gordons had found so distressing, no traveller saw any sign of it. Bishop Pococke's comment after his visit throughout the region in 1760 is not untypical. 'The people are in general extremely hospitable, charitable, civil, polite and sensible.' He was commenting on all classes of society, not merely the gentry. The social habits of all kinds of people, high and low, are described in the copious poetry of Rob Donn, without fear or favour, and the picture he has left is an attractive and creditworthy one.

The dress worn by the eighteenth Earl in his portrait by Allan Ramsay in the dining room at Dunrobin helps to explain this happy state of affairs. The youth of Sutherland and the Mackay Country were accustomed, by a tradition that went back to the raising of the Mackay Regiment in 1626, to serve a term of military service. It was not compulsory, though a delinquent might be put in the army as a punishment. It enabled the young to see the world beyond their village, introduced them to habits of discipline and put money in their pockets.

The kilted eighteenth Earl was Lieutenant Colonel of the Sutherland Fencible Regiment with a son of Lord Reay as his Major, when

Rob Donn the bard performed a period of service in 1760 and saw his portrait in Dunrobin:

Fhuair mi dhealbh air mo leth-taobh,
na sheasamh 'm breacan an fhèilidh.

I found his picture beside me, standing in his kilt and plaid.

In August 1760 a hundred of Lord Sutherland's Highlanders marched to Inveraray, where an observer commented: 'After a fatiguing march, they made as fine an appearance as any troops I ever beheld, and though they are but a young corps, there is scarce a regiment in his Majesty's service better disciplined.' Here is the ancient military clan organisation in modern dress, with the Sutherland Earl at its head. Most of the men in the ranks would have spoken only Gaelic. It is hard to believe that their Colonel had not learned to speak their language. It was, besides, the language of religion of a most devout people.

The Earl married Mary Maxwell, who bore him a daughter Elizabeth in 1765. The following year, when the Earl was only thirty-one years old, the two of them died of an epidemic while they were visiting Bath. Rob Donn, who was never sycophantic, expressed the grief of their people.

Is ann leamsa nach neònach an sluagh bhi brònach an Cataibh
O na chaill iad an lànan bha mìn, mòrdhalach, maiseach,
Iarla Uilleam an Còirneal 's a chèil'òg Màiri Macsual.

It is no wonder to me that folk are sorrowful in Sutherland,
Since they lost the couple who were harmonious,
magnificent, handsome,
Earl William the Colonel and his young spouse Mary Maxwell.

Like the succession of the earlier Elizabeth in 1508, that of their baby daughter was contested. There were the Sutherland claimants, who represented that the Gordons had obtained the earldom by criminal acts that could not be legalised by the passage of time. The Gordons of Gordonstoun maintained that under the infeftment of 1601 it was bound to pass to the nearest heir of the surname of Gordon. It is significant that none of the parties to the dispute mentioned the bogus Strathnaver title. The case dragged on until 1771 before the House of Lords decided in favour of the little Elizabeth.

Rob Donn expressed what may well have been the general attitude in her territories. The fire had been extinguished, he said, until only an ember remained.

Ach tha mi fathast an earbsadh am beagan aimsir an dèigh seo
Gum bi an t-sradag ud, Beataidh, na teine lasarach aoibhinn.

But I am still confident that in a little while from now
That spark, Betty, will blaze into a joyous fire.

The Countess Elizabeth was brought up, mainly in Edinburgh, by a Lowland grandmother, and did not visit Dunrobin until she was an adult. This was an age in which the ties between Chiefs and their Clans were weakening throughout the Highlands and Islands. MacLeod of Dunvegan in Skye was a spendthrift absentee of his own volition. It was not Elizabeth's fault that she had lost the parents who might have reared her in the country whose name she bore. But it had its inevitable consequences.

Of the portraits of the Countess Elizabeth at Dunrobin, John Hoppner's likeness has been admired especially. The husband whom she married in 1785 was praised two years later as 'a man of taste, virtue, reserved and very well bred'. His portraits at Dunrobin depict one who was also described as 'a dull, nervous man with a large, beaky nose and a prim mouth'. He was certainly shy and scholarly, liberal in his politics and heir to enormous wealth, though he had not yet inherited it at the time of his marriage.

It was said that the riches of the Leveson-Gowers stemmed from fortunate marriages rather than from innate abilities. The Gowers had been squires of Stittenham in Yorkshire since the Norman conquest. Thomas Gower, a baronet of 1620 creation, married the co-heiress of Sir John Leveson and acquired with her hand the seat of Trentham in Staffordshire and the wealth of the wool trade. Ennobled by Queen Anne as Tories, the Leveson-Gowers were promoted in the peerage in 1746 after they had switched from the Jacobite to the Hanoverian side in the uprising that ended at Culloden. Earl Gower, Viscount Trentham, married a sister of the heirless Duke of Bridgwater in 1748 and was created Marquess of Stafford. It was his son who married the Countess of Sutherland. 'A Leviathan of Wealth,' as he was described, he was Duke of Sutherland by the time of his death in 1833.

Such was the pair who spent their lives at the storm centre of public controversy over the Sutherland Clearances. These have remained ever since one of the most hotly debated occurrences in Scottish history. The removal of Gaelic tenants at will so that their lands could be leased to mainly Lowland sheep farmers was happening throughout the Highlands and Islands at this time, and this is not the place to discuss the subject. The most comprehensive examination of it has been published by the Australian historian Professor Eric Richards. His *The Leviathan of Wealth* appeared in 1973: his two-volume study *A History of the Highland Clearances* in 1982 and 1985.

The first Duke of Sutherland has been treated harshly. Sir Iain Moncreiffe wrote: 'Like so many reformers he was willing to devote his life and fortune to making other folk do something they found desparately disagreeable for the sake of what he believed to be their future good.' In saying this, Moncreiffe is attributing responsibility for the policy to the shy, rich Englishman, just as its victims did with more asperity.

> *Ciad Diùc Chataibh, le chuid foill,*
> *'S le chuid càirdeas do na Goill.*

> *First Duke of Sutherland, filled with deceit,*
> *Filled with liking for the Lowlanders.*

It was not fair to blame the future Duke because the estate managers and sheep farmers were generally Lowlanders, in Sutherland as elsewhere. In any case, his attitude was subservient to that of his domineering wife, whose views and character stand revealed in her own barely legible handwriting. As for his reaction when he paid his first visit to Dunrobin in 1787, it was observed: 'He does not like the bagpipe and says so and shows it indeed, for he has converted the piper into a porter. We may give the more credit to another declaration of his, that he likes Dunrobin and Sutherland as well as Staffordshire.' Those who reviled his disrespect for the piper might have recalled a Gaelic poem composed before his time, which expressed the same distaste in a most philistine manner.

The pair possessed so many homes, and were so accustomed to metropolitan life, that they could not spend a great deal of their time at Dunrobin. There was Lilleshall in Shropshire, Trentham in Staffordshire, and in London they purchased Stafford House opposite to Buckingham Palace in 1827, described by Professor Richards as the 'largest and most gorgeous of London's private palaces'. Today it is called Lancaster house, and is used as a government entertainment centre. The Marquess and Marchioness of Stafford, as they became in 1803, lived with a splendour that was the envy of royalty. Their fortune was derived from English canals and railways for the most part, and it appears to have been rather for considerations of status than on economic grounds that they bought up the remaining estates in Strathnaver from Mackay proprietors when they had the opportunity in 1829 and 1830 to become the greatest landowners in the kingdom, if not in Europe. It does not appear that they wished to give greater credence to the Strathnaver peerage title. When the Marquess was created a Duke, he had an earldom of his own apart from his wife's, and was a Viscount, Baron and Baronet as well.

When the second Duke succeeded in 1833, Charles Greville described his father as the 'richest individual who ever died'. He succeeded his mother as Earl of Sutherland on her death in 1839. Thomas Creevey called her a 'wicked old woman,' and those who study her life carefully may be forgiven for sharing his opinion.

> *Bhan Diùc Chataibh, bheil thu'd shith?*
> *Càit bheil nis do ghùntan sìod?*

> *Duchess of Sutherland, are you at rest?*
> *Where now are your silken gowns?*

The grounds for the execration with which this pair is remembered in Gaelic Scotland have been scoffed at by Edinburgh historians, and they may be right. But it is also right to recall the difference between Earl William the Colonel, who would only have been sixty-five years old by the end of the century had he not been cut off in his prime, and these rich, occasional visitors.

The second Duke did not inherit the Bridgwater fortune. It went to his younger brother who adopted the Bridgwater surname of Egerton, became Earl of Ellesmere, and commissioned Sir Charles Barry to build Bridgwater house in 1847. Barry had won a competition to rebuild the Palace of Westminster in 1836, which was opened formally by Queen Victoria in 1852. During the interval he also built three houses for the second Duke of Sutherland, one of them Dunrobin.

The astonishing versatility of this architect is revealed by the difference between all these buildings, the new Trentham, the gothic Houses of Parliament, the classical Cliveden, which the second Duke purchased in 1849 and asked Barry to remodel in 1850 after it had been seriously damaged by fire. In contrast with these, Dunrobin might be taken for a French château on the Loire.

Its entrance hall is filled with coloured armorials, enlivening the stonework, the stairway with Leveson-Gower portraits. While little remains to be seen of the older castle encased in Barry's building, so also much of Barry's interior work has been superseded. For Dunrobin was used as a hospital during the First World War and was damaged by fire in 1915. The work of restoration was entrusted to Sir Robert Lorimer, designer of the National War Memorial in Edinburgh Castle, and Dunrobin boasts some of his finest interiors.

The new panelled dining room, with its wall-top Italian frieze and light ribbed ceiling, is now the setting for Allan Ramsay's portrait of the kilted eighteenth Earl, as well as the Romney portrait of the first Marquess of Stafford whose son became Duke of Sutherland. The chairs contain the needlework of the fifth Duke's wife.

The great drawing room exemplifies the liberties that Lorimer took with Barry's original work, and how successfuly he did it. Here two rooms have been made into one, providing an ample gallery for the large Canalettos and eighteenth century tapestries, lit by a long line of windows that look down on the formal gardens which lie between the castle and the sea. Here hang the Hoppner and Reynolds portraits of the Countess Elizabeth, and the Phillip and Lawrence portraits of her son the second Duke. The library is another of Lorimer's achievements. Lined with sycamore wood, it frames the Lazlo portrait of Duchess Eileen, wife of the childless fifth Duke, who ornamented the dining chairs with her needle.

On the fifth Duke's death in 1963, another Countess succeeded in her own right. Unlike the first Elizabeth in 1508 or the second in 1766, the present Countess was the incontestable heir presumptive almost from her birth. Having her home in Sutherland long before she inherited Dunrobin, she enjoyed a respect and affection such as it would not have been easy for either of her earlier namesakes to earn. Her earldom was separated from all the other Leveson-Gower titles and properties, which passed with the dukedom in the male line to the fifth Earl of Ellesmere.

The Countess attempted first to transform Dunrobin into a boarding school for boys. It opened in 1965, but the venture lasted for only seven years. Now the castle and grounds are open to the public, while there are plans to develop the surrounding amenities in a manner that will provide recreation for visitors and a livelihood for local people.

It was a powerful blessing that Rob Donn invoked over two centuries ago, and it is being fulfilled at last.

INDEX

Picture credits:

Between pages 22 and 23: BBC ENTERPRISES (Tom Howatt) portrait of Niel Gow; J. ALLAN CASH Stirling exterior; HISTORIC BUILDINGS & MONUMENTS, EDINBURGH Stirling Chapel Royal; A. F. KERSTING Edinburgh – entrance and hall; WOODMANSTERNE Stirling – Douglas window and Palace, Atholl family portrait (Jeremy Marks), Blair – drawing room and dining room; ZEFA Blair exterior (F. Damm).

Between pages 54 and 55: BARNABY'S PICTURE LIBRARY Inveraray exterior; BBC ENTERPRISES (Tom Howatt) Inveraray – dining room, armoury, drawing room, Glamis sundial; NATIONAL TRUST FOR SCOTLAND painting of Culzean, Culzean – staircase (Stewart Guthrie) and saloon; PILGRIM PRESS, DERBY portraits of Duke of Argyll, Elizabeth Gunning and Earl of Strathmore's family; SPECTRUM Culzean and Glamis exteriors; WOODMANSTERNE Glamis – chapel and drawing room (Jeremy Marks).

Between pages 86 and 87: BBC ENTERPRISES (Tom Howatt) Craigievar – exterior and portrait of Forbes; NATIONAL TRUST FOR SCOTLAND Brodie – exterior, Red drawing room, Blue sitting room, ceiling, Craigievar – Queen's room, hall, Fyvie – exterior, hall, gallery, portrait of Isabella Macleod.

Between pages 118 and 119: BARNABY'S PICTURE LIBRARY Dunrobin exterior; BBC ENTERPRISES (Tom Howatt) Floors exterior; BRITISH TOURIST AUTHORITY painting of Floors, Floors – drawing room, portrait of Duchess May, ballroom (Barry Hicks), Dunrobin – drawing room, library, portrait (Barry Hicks); SCOTTISH TOURIST BOARD Thirlestane exterior; THIRLESTANE CASTLE TRUST Thirlestane drawing room; VICTORIA & ALBERT MUSEUM portrait of Duke of Lauderdale.